"But, seriously . . ."

DIE LAUGHING

KILLER JOKES
for
NEWLY OLD FOLKS

Selected and Annotated by

WILLIAM NOVAK

TOUCHSTONE
New York   London   Toronto   Sydney   New Delhi

Touchstone
An Imprint of Simon & Schuster, Inc.
1230 Avenue of the Americas
New York, NY 10020

First Touchstone hardcover edition October 2016

TOUCHSTONE and colophon are registered trademarks
of Simon & Schuster, Inc.

For information about special discounts for bulk purchases,
please contact Simon & Schuster Special Sales at 1-866-506-1949
or business@simonandschuster.com.

The Simon & Schuster Speakers Bureau can bring authors to
your live event. For more information or to book an event,
contact the Simon & Schuster Speakers Bureau at 1-866-248-3049
or visit our website at www.simonspeakers.com.

Interior design by Kyle Kabel

Manufactured in the United States of America

10   9   8   7   6   5   4   3

Library of Congress Cataloging-in-Publication Data

Names: Novak, William, editor.
Title: Die laughing : killer jokes for newly old folks / selected and
    annotated by William Novak.
Description: New York : Touchstone, 2016.
Identifiers: LCCN 2016016333| ISBN 9781501150791 (hardback) | ISBN
    9781501150807 (paperback)
Subjects: LCSH: Aging – Humor. | Old age – Humor. | BISAC:
    HUMOR / Form / Jokes & Riddles. | HUMOR / Topic / Marriage &
    Family. | FAMILY & RELATIONSHIPS / Aging.
Classification: LCC PN6231.A43 D49 2016 | DDC 818.602 – dc23 LC
    record available at https://lccn.loc.gov/2016016333

ISBN 978-1-5011-5079-1
ISBN 978-1-5011-5081-4 (ebook)

Is it possible to die from laughing?

It's an extremely rare occurrence, but it's been known to happen. In 1999, according to the *San Diego Union–Tribune*, a man in his thirties heard a joke in a Seattle bar that inspired a thirteen-hour laughing fit. The doctors were unable to stop his convulsions, and he died of heart failure. When the patient was asked what was so funny, he managed to say, between laughs, "There was something about an antelope. And shellfish. I remember a part about shellfish."

CONTENTS

DIE
LAUGHING

—

INTRODUCTION

Dad always thought laughter was the best medicine, which I guess is why several of us died of tuberculosis.

—Jack Handey

Although I'm not exactly old, I seem to be headed in that general direction. I was born in 1948, which brings up an important question: How much longer can I still pretend to be middle-aged?

Growing older was something that happened to my grandparents. Like so many of my fellow baby boomers, I thought our generation would remain forever young. Apparently we were misinformed. And now that I'm finally coming of age, I'm starting to experience some of the symptoms I've been hearing about for years, such as misplacing my car keys, forgetting names, and noticing various aches and pains that seem to have no rational explanation.

I've been vaguely aware that a growing number of the jokes that friends were telling me, or passing along over email, had to do with things like memory loss, Alzheimer's, long marriages, or other concerns of older people. Even so, I wasn't ready to acknowledge that any of this had much to do with me.

But all of these clues must have been loitering in my unconscious mind, because early in 2015 it suddenly occurred to me to compile a book of jokes about growing older. After all, I couldn't be the only one who would appreciate a chance to laugh about the approach of sixty, seventy, or some other significant birthday. So I started looking for jokes on age-related topics, and when I finally had enough, I selected the best ones, along with some wonderful cartoons, for this book.

Remember jokes? A priest, a minister, and a rabbi walk into a bar. Three nuns meet Saint Peter at the Pearly Gates. Although comedians stopped telling them long ago, jokes are still around, and one purpose of this book is to make sure they stay around.

With a sensitive subject like aging, it may be worth pointing out that jokes just don't portray the full scope of reality. They ignore a great deal that is true and reassuring because those things don't happen to be funny. And the point of jokes and cartoons, and certainly the point of this book, is to make you laugh.

Laughter may not be the best medicine, but a growing body of research is showing that it has some real health benefits:

It strengthens the immune system.

It relaxes the body and reduces stress.

It lowers blood pressure and increases blood flow.

Laughter also increases the ability to tolerate pain. This brings to mind Norman Cousins, longtime editor of the *Saturday Review*, who famously checked himself out of a hospital and into a hotel in the mid-1970s after being struck by an especially painful and life-threatening form of arthritis. After putting himself on a regimen of

Marx Brothers and television sitcoms, Cousins described "the joyous discovery that ten minutes of genuine belly laughter had an anesthetic effect that would give me at least two hours of pain-free sleep."

But wait – there's more. Much like exercise, laughter expands the blood vessels and helps prevent cardiovascular disease.

Some researchers think it may offset memory loss.

It releases endorphins, which improve a person's mood.

Laughter promotes optimism, which in turn improves resiliency.

It is also thought to stimulate learning, productivity, and problem solving.

And according to a seven-year study of more than fifty thousand Norwegians, older people with a sense of humor had a lower mortality rate than their counterparts who did not laugh easily at daily events.

Now, even if only half of these claims are actually true, the jokes in this collection should have a real health benefit. Of course, a lot of things have a real health benefit. But how many of them are this much *fun*?

The jokes that follow come from a variety of sources, including other books. (All joke books "borrow" from previous collections, although almost none of them admit it.) Some made their way to me from friends and fellow collectors, and others turned up on the internet, often in several different versions. In almost every case I have rewritten them. And all of the cartoons first appeared in the *New Yorker*.

A number of these jokes will be familiar, and I hope readers will greet them as old friends. Others, I trust, will be entirely new, and still others might strike the reader as completely wrong, because most people prefer the version of a joke that they already know.

None of the jokes carry an author's name because, unlike comic routines, one-liners, and cartoons, jokes don't have authors. As the legendary folklorist Gershon Legman observed in *Rationale of the Dirty Joke*, nobody has ever told a joke for the first time. Or, as the old saying goes, there are no new jokes — only new audiences.

Quotations do have authors, but a few of the one-liners in these pages have often been credited to the wrong people. (George Carlin was very talented, but he didn't come up with all the lines that are commonly ascribed to him.) Where it was impossible to determine the author of a quote with any certainty, no name is listed. Corrections from readers are welcome, but please be careful: "Don't believe everything you read on the internet just because there's a picture with a quote next to it." — Abraham Lincoln.

There are jokes and cartoons here about many things, including death. A certain amount of bad taste is unavoidable and even necessary in this book because life is full of bad taste. But I have mostly avoided crudeness, vulgarity, and four-letter words unless they were critical to the joke.

There are also jokes here that depend on wordplay. It's easy to disparage puns, or to treat all puns as bad puns, but I side with the satirist Jonathan Swift, who observed long ago that "punning is a talent which no man affects to despise but he that is without it."

Puns may also be good for you. "Wit and puns aren't just décor in the mind," writes Adam Gopnik. "They're essential signs that the mind knows it's on, recognizes its own software, and can spot the bugs in its own program."

I have introduced each chapter with a very short essay that I hope will provide some context and, from time to time, some cheerful news about the subject at hand. But if you'd prefer not to read anything serious in a book like this, be my guest.

When a character's age isn't mentioned, please assume that the person is no longer young, and in some cases may actually be old. And by "old," I mean a few years older than you are.

Finally, I decided to conclude each of the introductory essays, including this one, on a lighter note. I've put these jokes in italics so they'll be harder to miss.

———

When Larry's primary-care doctor referred him to a cardiologist, he thought the man's name sounded familiar. And when he showed up for his appointment and noticed the framed diploma on the wall, he recalled that a tall, dark-haired boy with that name had been in his high school class.

But when he met the doctor, he saw that although the names were the same, that was just a coincidence. This balding physician with a wrinkled face was clearly too old to have been his classmate.

Even so, he asked the doctor where he had gone to high school.

"I went to Memorial," the doctor said.

"So did I," said Larry. "And did you graduate in 1964?"

"How did you know?"

"You were in my class!"

"Really?" said the doctor. "What did you teach?"

"Hi. I'm, I'm, I'm . . . You'll have to forgive me,
I'm terrible with names."

TRY TO REMEMBER

Men forget everything; women remember everything. That's why men need instant replay in sports. They've already forgotten what's happened.

—Rita Rudner

I used to think that the brain was the most wonderful organ in my body. Then I realized who was telling me this.

—Emo Philips

Have you been forgetting things, such as a specific word that often eludes you, or the names of movies, books, restaurants, and especially people? If so, rest assured that you're perfectly normal.

Memory loss among people over sixty typically begins years earlier but progresses so gradually that it doesn't become apparent until it's impossible to ignore. Fortunately, only certain types of memory are affected. Explicit memory, as it's known, has to do with recalling specific details, such as the name of the person you met at that dinner, or where you left your gloves, or why you sometimes stand at the fridge with the door open because you can't recall what it was you wanted to take out – or put back in.

The other kind – implicit, or procedural, memory – is much less affected by age. This category includes the things you do almost automatically: driving a car, getting dressed, tying your shoes, or typing an email.

To put it another way, if you forget the name of your optician, or where you left your glasses, that's normal aging. But if you can't remember what *optician* means or that you *wear* glasses, that's far more serious.

Feeling better yet? This may help: an older person's most important mental functions, including judgment, wisdom, and the ability to give advice, may now be operating better than ever. It's not that younger people aren't capable of wisdom, but that's a gift we usually associate with chronological maturity. (How's that for a euphemism?)

During the 1984 presidential debates with Walter Mondale, Ronald Reagan was asked whether, at seventy-three, he was too old to be reelected. "I will not make age an issue of this campaign," he replied. "I am not going to exploit, for political purposes, my opponent's youth and inexperience." Even Mondale laughed at that one. (These days, of course, seventy-three doesn't sound all that old.)

Until recently, the most common fear of people over sixty was the prospect of developing cancer or heart disease. Although these two unwelcome visitors are still lurking around, the biggest worry these days is Alzheimer's, which has been called the greatest health threat of the twenty-first century. Fortunately, it's possible to lower the risk of developing Alzheimer's – or at least to delay it. One preventive measure is to remain in close contact with other people, because individuals with active and positive social networks are less likely to show signs of dementia.

Another line of defense is to build up what researchers

call "cognitive reserve," which is the mental equivalent of putting money aside for a rainy day. To increase the odds of maintaining a well-functioning mind, it's helpful to keep the brain active by learning a new and challenging skill such as another language, a new instrument, or a demanding game like chess or bridge. Learning a new *physical* skill, such as juggling or skiing, can change and strengthen the brain as well. Much like the body, the mind, too, needs ongoing sources of stress and stretching to continue to function at a high level.

It's becoming increasingly clear that the greatest benefits to the brain come from physical activity. Compared to their friends who remain sedentary, people who exercise – even if it's nothing more than a brisk daily walk – have a significantly lower risk of developing Alzheimer's or other forms of dementia. Exactly how exercise helps mental functioning isn't entirely clear, but it may have to do with stimulating the flow of blood, oxygen, and certain nutrients to the brain. And it could be that laughter is helpful in those same ways.

The first joke in this section, about the name of a restaurant, is one of my favorites. Apparently I'm not alone, because a number of people, when they heard that I was working on a book of jokes about getting older, couldn't wait to share it with me.

I'm also rather fond of this one:

———

A few years ago, at a state fair in Ohio, an older visitor noticed a sign that read: "Old Chief Thunder. Come into the tent and test his memory."

Unfortunately, the visitor's knowledge of Native American

culture was limited to the many TV Westerns he had watched as a boy. He entered the tent, turned to the elderly chief, raised his right hand, and said, "How."

"Good day," said the chief, ignoring the visitor's clumsy greeting. "What would you like to ask me?"

"Well, sir, what did you have for breakfast on July 19th, 1991?"

"Eggs," the chief replied. "Okay, who's next?"

A few years later, the same visitor was back at the fair, and again he saw the sign for Old Chief Thunder. He was surprised that the man was still alive, but he entered the tent and, just like last time, he greeted the chief by raising his right hand and saying "How."

"Fried," said the chief.

The Name of the Rose

A long-married couple are having dinner at the home of their good friends. When the meal has ended and the wives get up to clear the dishes, the men remain at the table and continue talking.

"I meant to tell you," says the host, "that we went to a terrific new restaurant on Thursday. I think you'll love it."

"Great. What's it called?"

"Damn, now I'm blanking. Help me out here. What's the name of that red flower?"

"A poppy?"

"No, the other one."

"A tulip?"

"No—you know, with thorns."

"A rose!"

"Thank you." Turning toward the kitchen, he yells, "Rose! What's the name of that restaurant?"

———

A popular version of this joke has the host raving about a memory school whose name he can't recall. But I prefer it this way, as the joke is strong enough without the added irony. (And also, I'm sure, because this is how I first heard it.)

What's in a Name?

A man walks into a pharmacy. "I'm looking for some acetylsalicylic acid," he tells the druggist.

"You mean aspirin?"

"Thank you! I can never remember that word."

Irrational Numbers

A doctor is sent to a nursing home to test the minds and memories of the residents. To save time, she interviews them in groups of three. The first group she meets with consists of three men.

Turning to the first one, she asks, "What's nine times thirteen?"

"That would be four hundred and six," the man replies.

Without giving any indication that his answer is wrong, she turns to the second man. "What do you think, sir? What's nine times thirteen?"

"That's easy," he says. "It's Thursday."

She turns to the third man and says, "Nine times thirteen?"

He answers immediately. "One hundred seventeen."

"Excellent," says the doctor. "How did you get it so quickly?"

"Simple," he says. "I just subtracted four hundred and six from Thursday."

The Pickup

An elderly gentleman, well dressed, nicely groomed, and rather handsome, walks into an upscale cocktail lounge. He sits down next to an elegant woman of a certain age and orders a drink. Turning toward her, he says, "So tell me, do I come here often?"

Unsafe at Any Speed

Two women on their way to the supermarket cruised right through a red light. The woman in the passenger seat was alarmed but said nothing. Five minutes later, they went through another red light. This time the passenger opened her mouth to speak, but she had been experiencing some confusion lately, so she again said nothing.

But when it happened a third time, she couldn't restrain herself. "Helen!" she cried. "Are you trying to get us killed? You've just gone through three red lights!"

"What?!" said Helen. "I thought *you* were driving!"

Terms of Endearment

Martin, a widower, was invited to dinner at the home of his old friends, John and Martha. During the course of the evening, he noticed that John, who was kind and affectionate to begin with, seemed even warmer than usual. Every time he addressed Martha, he called her Honey, Sweetheart, or Dear.

When Martha was away from the table, Martin leaned over and said, "John, I think it's wonderful that after all this time you still address your wife with such tenderness."

"I really do love her," said John. "But you and I are old friends, so I'll tell you the truth. For the past few years I've had trouble remembering her name."

———

When your memory goes, forget it!

At Your Service

Ronald and Andrea were watching TV one evening when Ronald got up and walked toward the kitchen.

"Honey, are you getting a snack?"

"Yes, I'm still hungry."

"Me, too."

"What would you like?"

"Vanilla ice cream."

"And would you like anything on that?"

"Good idea. How about strawberries and hot fudge sauce?"

"Coming right up."

"Hold on, honey. Don't you want to write that down? You know how you're forgetting things these days."

"Don't be silly! Vanilla ice cream with strawberries and hot fudge sauce."

Fifteen minutes later, Ronald returns to the living room with a plate of bacon and eggs.

"Thanks, honey," she tells him. "But you should have written it down. You forgot the toast!"

Trading Places

Two old friends are having lunch. Over coffee, one of them says, "Arlene, I know this sounds ridiculous, but every time I look at you I think I see a suppository in your ear."

"Very funny," says Arlene. But when she checks her ear, sure enough, she finds a suppository.

"Well, what do you know? But I guess there's a good side to this. I think I know where I put my hearing aid."

*"Am I the smart one and you're the pretty one
or is it the other way around?"*

Who's Who

Frank Sinatra goes to see his mother in a nursing home. It's his first visit, and the residents are thrilled to see him.

He patiently answers their questions and signs a few autographs. When he notices a woman who is sitting alone and paying no attention to him, a mixture of compassion and narcissism prompts him to go over and sit with her.

"How are you today?" he says.

"Not too bad," she replies. "Are you here to visit someone?"

"Yes, my mother lives here. By the way, do you have any idea who I am?"

"No," says the woman, "but if you go to the front desk, I'm sure they can tell you."

A Real Puzzle

A woman who is getting on in years calls her daughter. "Judy, can you come over and give me a hand?"

"Sure, Mom. What's the problem?"

"This jigsaw puzzle I'm working on is just impossible. I'm normally very good at these, but this one's driving me crazy."

"Sure, Mom, I'll come after lunch. What's the puzzle supposed to look like when it's done?"

"How should I know?"

"Well, what's the picture on the box?"

"It's a big rooster."

When the daughter arrives and sees the pieces spread out all over the table, she says, "Mom, I don't think we're going to get this one."

"But I've always been good at puzzles. Just help me get started."

"Well, first I'm going to make you a nice cup of tea."

"And then?"

"And then we'll put all the cornflakes back in the box."

Feeling His Age

Maurice was proudly telling everyone in assisted living that today was his birthday.

Alice came up to him and said, "Happy birthday, Maurice. Would you like me to guess your age?"

"Sure, why not?"

"Okay," said Alice. "Pull down your pants."

The birthday boy complied, and Alice fondled his genitals for a good half a minute. "Maurice," she said, "I do believe that you're eighty-six."

"You're right! How did you figure that out?"

"You told me yesterday."

Identity Crisis

Two women, old friends who hadn't seen each other in ages, happened to meet on the street. After chatting for a while, one of them said, "This is embarrassing, and I hope you won't think I'm rude, but my memory is spotty these days. I know a hundred things about you, but for some reason I'm blanking on your name."

Her friend paused in thought for a long moment and said, "How soon do you need to know?"

———————

Right now I'm having amnesia and déjà vu at the same time. I think I've forgotten this before.

—Steven Wright

Let There Be Light

A man goes to the doctor for a checkup. "You look perfectly healthy to me," says the doctor. "How are you feeling these days?"

"I feel fine," the man says, "and the Lord has been good to me. Every night when I get up to go to the bathroom, He turns the light on. And when I'm finished, He turns it off."

Not knowing what to make of this answer, the doctor sends the patient to have his blood drawn and asks the man's wife to come in from the waiting room. He tells her that her husband seems to be in good shape and mentions what he said about the bathroom light.

"What's this about?" the doctor asks. "Is he really that religious?"

"No," she says. "It means he's peeing in the fridge again."

Forgetful Jones

Two older men, acquaintances but not really friends, are sitting on a park bench.

One turns to the other and says, "Remind me, was it you or your brother who died last winter?"

———

When my friend Jerry told me this one, I knew immediately that I had to include it. A few weeks later, at a used book sale in Vermont, I came across a slim volume called The World's Oldest Joke Book. It's a translation of a Greek document known as Philogelos, which consists of a couple of hundred jokes from the fourth century. I was delighted and more than a little surprised that Jerry's joke was in there among so many others that have deservedly been forgotten over the years. In the earlier version the brothers are twins, which may be even better.

Knock Knock

Three older women are having lunch together. The first one says, "I've become so forgetful! Why, just yesterday I was standing in front of the fridge with a bottle of milk in my hand, and I couldn't remember whether I was taking it out or putting it back."

The second one says, "I know what you mean. The other day I was standing at the top of the stairs, and I couldn't remember whether I had just come up or was about to go down."

"I guess I'm lucky," says the third woman, "because my memory is as good as it's always been, knock on wood." She raps twice on the table, looks up, and says, "Someone's at the door. I'd better go answer it."

Ups and Downs

A man says to his doctor: "I'm afraid I'm getting senile. Sometimes, when I pee, I forget to zip up."

"That's nothing to be concerned about," says the doctor. "Call me when you forget to zip down."

———

At my age, it's a good day when I zip my fly and my schmeckle's on the right side of the zipper.

A Good Match

They had known each other forever, and each of them had recently lost their longtime spouse. Now, at their sixtieth high school reunion, they were inseparable.

As the evening was winding down, Ed got up the courage to propose. "Carol, I know this is rather sudden, but will you marry me?"

"Ed, I would love to," she replied.

Ed went home in a wonderful mood. But the next morning, although he remembered the proposal, he couldn't recall Carol's response. Had she actually said yes? He thought so, but he wasn't sure. Did she want time to think about it? Or had she conceivably turned him down?

With great anxiety, he picked up the phone and called her. Apologizing for his faulty memory, he said, "Last night, when I asked you to marry me, what did you say?"

"Oh, Ed, I said yes, and I meant it with all my heart."

"That's what I thought," he said. "I'm so pleased – and relieved, too, of course."

"I was hoping I'd hear from you today," said Carol, "because I remember the proposal, and I remember saying yes. But for the life of me, I just couldn't recall who had asked me."

We Meet Again

At their twentieth college reunion, a group of men in their forties decided to have dinner together. After a lot of discussion, they made a reservation at Chez Paris because the food was excellent and the waitresses wore low-cut blouses.

They had such a wonderful time that they decided to have dinner together at every major college reunion.

Ten years later, in their fifties, they decided to meet again at Chez Paris because the food was so good and the wine list was outstanding.

In their sixties they decided to meet once again at Chez Paris because the restaurant was quiet and smoke-free.

In their seventies they decided to meet yet again at Chez Paris because it offered a senior discount and was wheelchair accessible.

In their eighties, they decided to eat at Chez Paris because they heard the food was good and they wanted to try someplace new.

Get Back

An older man walked into a bar, ordered a beer, and started crying.

"What's the matter?" asked the bartender. "Why are you so unhappy?"

"Well," sniffed the customer, "a few days ago I married a lovely young woman who's twenty-eight. She's beautiful, she's smart, she's sexy as hell, she loves to watch football, and she's a wonderful cook. She didn't marry me for my money because she has more than I do. We have a wonderful time together, and we really love each other."

"That's wonderful!" says the bartender. "It sounds like every man's dream. So why are you crying?"

"I forget where we live!"

No Direction Home

Brendan was driving home when his wife called.

"Honey, are you on the turnpike?"

"Yes."

"Well, be careful! I just heard on the radio that some maniac is driving in the wrong direction."

"It's not just one maniac. It's hundreds of them!"

––––––––

This one brings to mind an old adage: If somebody calls you a jackass, ignore them. But if three people call you a jackass, you might want to get a saddle.

"Hmm — I don't like the looks of that eye."

OUR BODIES, OURSELVES

My face has been tucked in more times than a
bedsheet at the Holiday Inn.

—Joan Rivers

I don't feel like an old man. I feel like a young
man who has something the matter with him.

—Bruce Bliven

Everybody knows that the human body changes with
age, and generally not for the better. Fortunately,
many of these changes are manageable, although a few
are beyond control: baldness in many men, a slight loss
of height, and, of course, wrinkles. Fortunately, none of
these is painful – at least not physically.

Weight gain is common after middle age, but it can
usually be overcome by self-discipline, conscientious
eating, and physical activity. And although your muscles
lose some of their strength, free weights and weight-
bearing workouts can help enormously. Reduced bone
density makes falls more dangerous, but here, too, lifting
weights or using the machines at any gym can make a
big difference.

The various senses change as well. Happily, most people

find that their sense of humor remains intact, which is a good thing because they'll certainly be needing it. Most vision problems are correctible with prescription glasses, so let's raise one – a glass, I mean – to Ben Franklin for inventing bifocals. But it's important to stay up to date. "I was walking down the street wearing my eyeglasses," says comedian Steven Wright, "when all of a sudden my prescription ran out."

Hearing loss is a more serious problem, especially among men. As with eyesight, most hearing issues are correctible, but not as easily or inexpensively. And many men who could benefit from a hearing aid fail to buy one: either they don't realize how much their hearing has declined, or they refuse to acknowledge the problem because it undermines their self-image and their vanity. Those in the second group may not realize that their auditory limitations are far more apparent to friends and family members than any hearing aid would be.

People with significant and untreated hearing loss miss significant chunks of social interaction, which affects not only their relationships, but their minds as well. In some cases, untreated hearing loss can hasten dementia.

Moving downstairs and around the corner brings us to a very different issue. People over sixty lose elasticity and muscle tone just about everywhere, including where the sun don't shine. And if they're consuming a lot of healthful, high-fiber vegetables and fruit such as broccoli, cabbage, cauliflower, salads, and apples, not to mention beans, there may be consequences. Some prescription medications have a similar effect.

Farts have always been considered funny, and humor about flatulence has a long and, yes, distinguished history. Aristophanes, Chaucer, Dante, and Shakespeare all included fart jokes in their works, and children from four to a hundred and four continue to find them amusing.

Farting, hearing loss, and erectile dysfunction account for many of the jokes in this section. And what about all those trips to the bathroom in the middle of the night? Fortunately, help may be on the way:

———

Vintners in California's Napa Valley, which is known for such varieties as Pinot Blanc, Pinot Noir, and Pinot Grigio, have been experimenting with a new hybrid grape that is designed to reduce the number of times older people have to get up in the night to use the bathroom. If these efforts are successful, the new wine will be known as Pinot More.

Stayin' Alive

At their fortieth high school reunion, Dwight runs into Jonesy, his old classmate. "You look absolutely amazing," Dwight says. "You don't seem to have aged at all."

"Thanks, I hear that all the time. I guess looking young runs in our family."

"Did your father live a long life?"

"Who says he died? He's eighty-two, and still running marathons."

"Unbelievable! How old was your grandfather when he died?"

"Who says he died?"

"You don't mean to tell me – "

"Yes, Grampa is still with us, and every morning he walks five miles before breakfast. Not only that, but next week he's getting married again."

"You can't be serious. How old is your grandfather?"

"He's a hundred and three."

"That's incredible. But why would a man that age want to get married?"

"Because his parents keep nagging him."

Tommy, Can You Hear Me?

At the end of his annual physical, Thomas mentions that he's concerned about his wife, who seems to be experiencing some hearing loss.

"I'll be happy to meet with her," says the doctor. "But before you bring her in, try this simple test to see how serious the problem might be. Stand about thirty feet behind her and ask her a question in your normal speaking voice. If she doesn't answer, ask her again from twenty feet, and then ten. And if she still doesn't answer, go up right behind her and ask her again."

When Thomas gets home, his wife is in the kitchen, facing the stove. From thirty feet away, he says, "Honey, what's for dinner?" No response.

Coming a little closer, he asks again: "Honey, what's for dinner tonight?" Again, no response.

And closer still. And even now, no reply.

Finally, he comes up right behind her and says, "Honey, what's for dinner tonight?"

His wife turns around and says, "For the fourth time – we're having chicken!"

Moving On Up

Some years ago, when she was in her fifties, Margaret had gone to see a plastic surgeon. Instead of surgery, he fitted her with a new and experimental device known as The Dial. Implanted discreetly on the top of her head, this ingenious little instrument allowed Margaret to tighten her skin as much or as little as she wished.

She loved the device, which had served her well for twenty years. But now she went back to the doctor. "I've been very happy with The Dial," she said. "It's helped me enormously, but two weeks ago it stopped working. There are large bags under my eyes, but I can't turn the knob any further."

"I see what you mean," said the doctor. "But those aren't bags. You've tightened the knob so often over the years that what appear to be bags under your eyes are actually your breasts."

"Oh, my," Margaret said. After pausing for a moment to let this new information sink in, she added, "So I guess that explains the goatee."

———

My breasts are so low, now I can have a mammogram and a pedicure at the same time.

—Joan Rivers

Downright Upright

It was a difficult decision, but the siblings finally and reluctantly moved their elderly mother into a nursing home.

The youngest daughter returned the next day to see how she was doing. She found her mother sitting in the garden and decided to watch from a distance before speaking with her. Soon the older woman started to lean slightly to one side. Without missing a beat, two attendants rushed over and straightened her up.

As soon as they left, she started to lean slightly to the other side. Again, the attendants ran over and straightened her up. This pattern continued, with the woman leaning first to one side and then the other, and the attendants rushing over to straighten her.

Finally, the daughter went over to her mother and said, "Mom, how are you doing?"

"Well, as you know, I wasn't crazy about coming here, but there's a lot to like," she says. "The garden is beautiful, the food is good, I've already made a couple of friends, and the staff is very nice. There's just one problem."

"And what's that?"

"They won't let you fart."

Morning Joe

A woman goes to consult her doctor about reviving her husband's libido.

"I'll give you some Viagra," he says.

"Thanks, but he'll never take it. Joe hates pills."

"In that case," says the doctor, "when Joe's not looking, drop one in his morning coffee. He won't even know it's there. Call me next week and let me know if it helped."

When the woman calls, the doctor says, "So how did our little experiment work out?"

"We had mixed results," she says. "The pill worked immediately. Within minutes, he leaped to his feet, tore off my dress, and made love to me right there on the table."

"That's wonderful," says the doctor. "So what was the problem?"

"I'm pretty sure they'll never let us into that particular Starbucks again."

Smell Ya Later

A woman goes to her doctor and confesses to an embarrassing situation. "I've been passing a lot of gas lately. These are silent farts. They don't smell, but they're annoying. Last night, at dinner with friends, it happened throughout the meal. It's also happening right now, while we're talking."

"I'm going to give you a prescription," the doctor says. "Take one of these pills three times a day, and come back to see me in two weeks."

When the woman returns, she says, "I don't know what's in those pills. I'm farting just as much, but now, instead of being odorless, they've become unbearably smelly."

"Okay," says the doctor. "Now that we've cleared up your sinuses, we can get to work on your hearing."

———

A different version: When the woman announces that her farts are frequent but odorless, the doctor goes over to his instrument case. "Are you going to operate on my butt?" she asks.

"No," he replies. "I'm going to operate on your nose."

———

Why do farts smell?
So deaf people can enjoy them, too.

Hear, Hear

Frank hadn't been hearing well for years, but he stubbornly refused to do anything about it. Only when it became unbearable did he go to the doctor, who fitted him with a pair of tiny hearing aids that were almost invisible.

"Come back in thirty days," the doctor said, "and we'll make the necessary adjustments."

When Frank returned, the doctor ran a few tests and said, "Your hearing shows a terrific improvement. Your family must be thrilled that you can hear like you used to."

"My family?" said Frank. "I haven't told them yet. In the past month, I've changed my will three times."

———

Given the emotional complications associated with wills, which should make them a popular subject for humor, there are surprisingly few jokes about them. One old chestnut that springs immediately to mind describes the reading of a will in a lawyer's office with the whole family present, and ends with, "And for my nephew, Dennis, whom I promised to remember in my will: hello there, Dennis!"

The Real Scoop

A little old man hobbled into the ice cream parlor and slowly made his way to the counter. After pausing a moment to catch his breath, he ordered a chocolate sundae.

"Crushed nuts?" asked the waitress.

"No. Arthritis."

———

I don't deserve this award, but I have arthritis and I don't deserve that either.

—Jack Benny

Double Trouble

Albert's wife drove him to the optician so he could pick up his new glasses. "These lenses will take some getting used to," the optician said. "For a day or so they'll feel all wrong because your new prescription is much stronger, but in a couple of days they'll feel just right."

On the way home they stopped at a restaurant for lunch. "Honey," said Albert, "I can't read the menu because I'm seeing double, so please order me a tuna melt while I go to the men's room."

When Albert returned, the front of his pants was all wet. "What happened to you?" his wife asked.

"It's these new glasses," he said. "I was standing at the urinal, and when I looked down, I saw two. So I put one of them back."

On the Road

Four residents of a retirement home are discussing their respective ailments.

"My cataracts are so bad that I'm close to blind," says one man.

"I'm having a terrible time with my hearing," a woman chimes in.

"My blood pressure pills make me dizzy," says another.

"Well," says the fourth, "I guess that's the price we pay for getting old. But let's count our blessings. At least we can all still drive."

———

Retirement at sixty-five is ridiculous. When I was sixty-five I still had pimples.

—George Burns

The Endorsement

Two old friends meet on the street. "Jim, how are you?"

"I'm doing well, thanks. I just bought a new hearing aid, and I'm loving it."

"I didn't even notice, so it must be small – and it was probably expensive."

"It was," says Jim, "but it's worth it. This little gizmo uses the latest technology. I couldn't live without it."

"Is that right?" says the friend. "Maybe I should get one. What kind is it?"

"A quarter to three."

The Makeover

Roger had just turned seventy, and after many selfless years of helping others while neglecting his own health and appearance, he finally resolved to take better care of himself. He became a vegetarian and paid close attention to nutrition. He exercised vigorously every day and lost thirty pounds. He bought clothes that looked good on him and splurged on an expensive haircut.

A few weeks later, while crossing the street, he was hit by a bus. Lying on the side of the road and knowing that this was the end, he cried out, "Lord, how could you do this to me?"

A voice answered back. "Roger? I'm so sorry! I didn't recognize you!"

I don't exercise. If God had wanted me to bend over, he would have put diamonds on the floor.

—Joan Rivers

Escalation

A retired man tells his doctor that he's been wetting his bed at least twice a week.

The doctor asks, "On nights when this happens, do you have any dreams?"

"Yes, how did you know? I have a dream in which a little demon appears to me and says, 'Let's pee.'"

"Well," says the doctor, "the next time the demon appears to you, I want you to say, 'No thanks, we've already peed.'"

A few days later, the man returns.

"Did you follow my advice?"

"I certainly did."

"And did it help?"

"No, it made things worse."

"How do you mean?"

"When I said, 'We've already peed,' the demon nodded and said, 'Okay, then, let's shit a little.'"

A Hard Choice

A woman runs into her old friend at the mall.

"Anything new in your life?"

"Yes, but you'll never believe me."

"Go on."

"Well, when I was gardening the other day I found an old lamp. I rubbed it and out popped a genie."

"And he gave you three wishes?"

"That's what I expected, but he explained very nicely that most genies don't have that much power, and that he was authorized to give me a choice between one of two wishes. He could give me a better memory, or he could endow my husband with a bigger and more reliable you-know-what."

"Tough choice! So which one did you choose?"

"That's the funny thing. I can't remember!"

Soup's On

A woman goes to see her doctor about her husband's flagging libido.

"Well, by now he must have tried Viagra," says the doctor, "so should we consider some other medication?"

"No, he hasn't tried anything. He hates pills. He won't even take an aspirin."

"Does he have a favorite kind of soup?"

"He loves chicken noodle. Why do you ask?"

"I'll give you a Viagra pill. Crush it up into powder and add it to his soup. He'll never know it's there."

That night, she makes chicken noodle soup and adds in the crushed-up Viagra.

As they sit down to dinner, her husband is looking at the soup but not touching it.

"Is something wrong with the soup?" she asks.

"I'm sure it's fine," he says. "I'm just waiting for the noodles to settle down."

The marketers of Viagra have a new slogan, "Let the Dance Begin." This is much better than the original, "Brace Yourself, Grandma!"

—Jay Leno

I'll Have What He's Having

The old farmer asked the vet to examine his prized bull.

"What seems to be the problem?" the vet asked.

"In the past couple of weeks he won't even look at a cow."

"I see," said the vet. "I'll give you some pills. Put two or three of them into his feed every day, and in a few days he should be back to normal."

A week later, the farmer's neighbor said, "What's going on with that bull of yours? I've never seen him so active!"

"Yes, it's really something. The vet gave him some pills and they're working awfully well."

"What kind of pills?"

"I don't know what they're called," said the farmer, "but they have a strong minty taste."

Another Viagra Joke

Two men in an assisted-living facility are talking about their health. "I know I'm behind the times," says one. "But for years I've been hearing people talk about Viagra. Tell me, is it everything they say?"

"I don't know what you've heard," says his friend, "but it's pretty amazing. Some people call it the fountain of youth."

"Well, if I go to a drugstore, could I get it over the counter?"

"I'm not sure," says his friend. "That might require more than one pill."

———

I went to my doctor and told him, "My penis is burning." He said, "That means somebody is talking about it."
                                        —Garry Shandling

"All this talk of Viagra and penile implants reminds me of a charming story about my own penis."

The Amazing McGregor

Two brothers are vacationing in a small Florida town. The beach is beautiful and they both love to swim, but there's nothing to do when the sun goes down. One evening they see a banner: "Tonight Only. Don't Miss the Amazing McGregor at Town Hall Auditorium."

So of course they buy tickets and go to the show. The program begins with a singer, who is followed by a comedian. Then, after a trumpet fanfare, a spotlight illuminates a table with three walnuts on it. An older man in a kilt comes out and stands silently at the table. He nods to the audience, lifts up his kilt, and takes hold of his most private part. Then, with three mighty swings — *Bam! Bam! Bam!* — he destroys each of the walnuts. As the Amazing McGregor bows and leaves the room, the audience responds with cheers and thunderous applause.

Twenty years later, the brothers spend another week in that same town. To their astonishment, they come across the very same banner announcing that the Amazing McGregor will be at Town Hall that very evening.

"Shall we see him again?" one brother asks.

"Is that even a question?" says the other. "We've been telling everybody about this guy for twenty years, and now he's a lot older. I'm surprised he's still alive, and I can't believe he's strong enough to do it again."

"You're right," says the first brother. "We've got to go."

This time the warm-up acts feature a younger singer and a different comedian. And instead of walnuts on the table, there are three coconuts. When the Amazing McGregor appears, he once again takes out his mighty member. *Bam! Bam! Bam!* He demolishes the coconuts one by one.

"We've got to meet this guy," one brother says, so they wait for McGregor to come out of his dressing room. When he finally appears, they go up to him and say, "That was quite a show you put on! Do you do this every night?"

"Six nights a week," says McGregor. "During the winter months, I try to visit every venue in Florida."

"We saw you perform twenty years ago, when you did your act with walnuts. But now you're using coconuts. Can I ask why?"

"Well," says the performer, "after all this time, my eyesight ain't what it used to be."

———

My parents didn't want to move to Florida, but they turned sixty, and that's the law.

—Jerry Seinfeld

*"This is a second opinion.
At first, I thought you had something else."*

DOCTORS

Is there a doctor in the house? My parents want me to marry you.

—Wendy Liebman

I told my doctor I broke my leg in two places. He told me to quit going to those places.

—Henny Youngman

If you enjoy complaining, the medical profession offers oodles of opportunities: how many weeks (or even months) it can take to get an appointment, followed by all that time in the doctor's waiting room; the expensive tests that may feel unnecessary (and sometimes are); the brevity of a typical office visit; or a diagnosis that's exasperating in its vagueness.

On a deeper level, some patients, knowingly or not, may resent the fact that to the doctor, they're just one more name on her daily schedule. Although their problem may not be serious, it certainly *feels* serious. As Mel Brooks famously observed, "Tragedy is when I cut my finger. Comedy is when you fall into an open sewer and die."

I'm reasonably sure that the great majority of doctors

do the best they can, and that some of their patients – not you or me, of course, but a few of those other people in the waiting room – can be demanding and unrealistic. And I like to remind myself that I'm blessed to be living in an era of unprecedented medical advancement. Consider, for example, that something as essential as penicillin was discovered as recently as 1928 and wasn't widely used until the 1940s, or that some of the other near-miraculous innovations in twentieth-century medicine are already out of date.

Of course, that still leaves plenty to grumble about – and, more important, to laugh about. After all, doctors often see patients at their most vulnerable – when they're sick, in pain, or in desperate need of answers that can be difficult to find. And when you add in the imbalance between a doctor in a white coat and a patient in a ridiculous robe, you end up with an ideal setting for humor and satire.

Because doctors play such an important role in the lives of many older people, the characters in these jokes and cartoons aren't necessarily members of the senior class. But it's safe to assume that at least some of the patients have a little wear on their tires.

What strikes me about the jokes in this section is that in almost all of them, the doctor comes off looking good. Authority figures don't normally fare that well in jokes, so this may indicate that for all their frustrations, most patients are grateful for the medical care they receive. And perhaps they're willing to grant doctors at least some of the compassion they hope and expect doctors will give to them.

Something to Sneeze At

"It's just a bad cold," the doctor said. "And as you know, there's no cure for that. You'll just have to wait it out for a few days."

"But it's making me miserable. There must be *something* I can do."

"Well, you could go home and take a hot bath. Then open all the windows and stand for a while in the cold air."

"But wouldn't I get pneumonia?"

"You might. But for that we have a cure."

———

Some readers may object that only bacterial pneumonia can be cured, whereas viral pneumonia goes away on its own. But hey, it's just a joke.

My Son, the Plumber

When a pipe burst in Dr. Benson's house, he called a plumber, who arrived within the hour.

After banging around in the basement for a few minutes, the plumber came up and told the doctor that the problem had been fixed.

"Great," said the doctor. "How much do I owe you?"

"Three hundred dollars."

"Three hundred dollars for fifteen minutes? I'm a doctor, and I don't make that kind of money."

"I know," said the plumber. "I didn't either when I was a doctor."

The Going Rate

A woman goes to a psychiatrist.

"So, what brings you here today?" he asks.

"Well, I think I'm a nymphomaniac."

"I can help you with that," says the psychiatrist. "My rate is three hundred dollars an hour."

"That's about what I expected," she says. "And how much for all night?"

Our Promise to You

"I'm a little nervous," the patient tells the nurse. "Just last week I read about a man who was being treated for heart disease and then died of pneumonia."

"You've got nothing to worry about," says the nurse. "This is a first-rate hospital. When we treat somebody for heart disease, he dies of heart disease."

———

The worst time to have a heart attack is during a game of charades.

—Demetri Martin

"The ringing in your ears — I think I can help."

Tunnel Vision

A man has been referred to a proctologist. When the nurse shows him in, he says, "This is my first time here, so I'm a little nervous."

"I'm sure you'll be fine," she says. "And we have something in common. Today is my first day on the job, so this will be a learning experience for both of us."

She shows him into the exam room, hands him a hospital gown, and says the doctor will be with him shortly.

As the man is waiting, he sees three items lined up on the counter: a jar of Vaseline, a rubber glove, and a bottle of beer.

When the doctor finally comes in, the man says, "Doc, this is my first time here, and I'm a little confused. I understand the jelly and the glove, but why is there a bottle of beer?"

The doctor just shakes his head. Then he opens the door and yells, "Damnit, Amy, I said a *butt* light."

———

Twinkle, twinkle, little star.
Why's his finger up so far?

A Doctor in the House

A doctor is relaxing with his wife after dinner when his phone rings. "Are you available?" a colleague asks. "Dave had an emergency and we need a fourth for poker."

"You need me now? Okay, I'll be right there."

"Is it serious?" his wife asks.

"It must be," he says. "They have three doctors there already."

Waits and Measures

She liked her doctor, but she hated those long delays before her name was called.

When she was finally brought in, the nurse led her to the scale and said, "I just need to record your weight."

"Sure," said the woman. "It was an hour and six minutes."

––––––––

They say time is a great healer. Maybe that's why they make you wait so long at the doctor's office.

Special Delivery

A man goes to the doctor because he's convinced that something painful is stuck up his butt.

The doctor examines him and can't find anything.

"Are you sure?" says the patient. "I'm pretty sure there's something in there."

"I could probe a little deeper if you'd like," says the doctor.

"I think you should," the patient says.

"Aha!" says the doctor. "You're right! There's a reason your butt was hurting."

"What did you find?"

"You won't believe this, but I just pulled out a dozen long-stemmed roses! Do you have any idea how they got there?"

"Keep looking. Maybe there's a card!"

———

There's an alternative punch line, which my friend Jeff prefers: The patient, responding to the doctor's question of how the roses got there, says, "I have no idea. Read the card!" In Jeff's version—and he's the one who told me the joke—the patient assumes there's a card, and the only question is, Who sent the flowers?

Health Insurance

Victor, who was close to eighty, was in the hospital for a serious operation. But he agreed to have it only if it was performed by his son, a respected surgeon.

Just before the anesthesiologist came in, the patient asked for a word with the surgeon.

"Yes, Dad?"

"Don't be nervous, Ted. Just do your best. And I want to remind you that if anything should happen to me, your mother will be moving in with you and Janice."

The Hypochondriac

"You really don't need me to come to the house," the doctor tells Mrs. Miller. "I've been treating your husband for years, and he isn't really sick. He just *thinks* he's sick."

Two days later, Mrs. Miller calls the doctor again.

"And how is your husband today?" he asks.

"He's worse."

"In what way?"

"He thinks he's dead."

———

This one brings to mind the well-known tombstone inscription "I told you I was sick." It's also an unusual example of a joke where the doctor turns out to be wrong.

You Light Up My Wife

A woman goes to a psychiatrist and says, "Would you be willing to see my husband?"

"Certainly. What seems to be the problem?"

"He thinks he's a refrigerator."

"Well, that's a harmless delusion. Give it time, and it will probably pass."

"I can't wait that long," she says. "He sleeps with his mouth open, and the light is keeping me up."

The Referral

A man goes to see a urologist. "My penis is full of holes," he says.

"What do you mean?"

"Well, there are six or seven holes along the length of it, and when I urinate, it's always a big mess because it sprays in all directions. Honestly, Doc, it's like a watering can."

"Let's have a look at you," says the doctor. The man undresses, and sure enough, his penis really *is* full of holes.

The doctor writes a name and a phone number on a piece of paper and hands it to the patient.

"Is this guy a specialist?" the patient says.

"He's a clarinet teacher. He can show you how to hold it."

Adaptation

"Mrs. Taylor," says the doctor, "I have some very bad news. You have rabies. I wish you had come to me earlier, but at this point you don't have much time left."

Mrs. Taylor, who is clearly in shock, stands up and leaves without a word.

A few minutes later, the doctor sees her in the waiting room, where she's writing something on a sheet of paper.

"Are you preparing your will?" he asks.

"No," she says. "I'm making a list of all the people I'm going to bite."

———

Doctors can drive you crazy. You wait weeks for an appointment, and when you show up, they say, "I wish you'd come to me sooner."

Timing

The test results had come in and the news wasn't good. So when the doctor called, he couldn't offer much comfort. "Sam, I'm sorry to say that I have bad news and worse news."

Sam was speechless, so the doctor continued. "The bad news is that you have twenty-four hours to live."

"That's terrible," said Sam. "But what can possibly be worse than that?"

"I forgot to call you yesterday."

———

With my doctor, I don't get no respect. I told him, "I've swallowed a bottle of sleeping pills." He told me to have a few drinks and get some rest.

—Rodney Dangerfield

A Time to Worry

Shortly before her operation, the patient ran out of the surgical unit and found her husband in the waiting room. "Let's get out of here," she said.

"Why, what's the matter?"

"The nurse was saying that this is a simple procedure, that there was nothing to worry about, and that everything would be fine."

"That's true, so what's the problem?"

"She was talking to the surgeon."

———

I had surgery last year. Nothing serious, thank God. But just before I went under, I heard the one thing you don't want to hear in that situation: "Where's my lucky scalpel?"

—Jonathan Katz

A Hole in One

A dentist was examining a new patient. "Oh, my!" he said. "That's the biggest cavity I've ever seen. The biggest cavity I've ever seen."

"Was that really necessary?" asked the patient.

"What do you mean?"

"I'm frightened enough as it is. Why did you repeat yourself about the size of the cavity?"

"I didn't," said the dentist. "That was the echo."

———

And then there's the Buddhist who refused to let the dentist give him Novocain because he was hoping to transcend dental medication.

Information, Please

An older lady calls the hospital switchboard. "Can you please help me get an update on one of your patients?"

"I'll certainly try, ma'am. What's the patient's name?"

"Denise McCarthy in room 716."

"If you don't mind waiting, I'll check with the nursing station on that floor."

"Thank you. I can wait."

Three minutes later, the switchboard operator says, "Thanks for your patience. Mrs. McCarthy is progressing nicely. Her blood work came back normal, her blood pressure is good, and they expect to discharge her tomorrow."

"Thank you. That's wonderful news. I was so worried."

"I'm guessing you're Denise's sister, or maybe a close friend?"

"No, I'm Denise. And I'm calling because nobody here tells me a damn thing!"

Good News, Bad News

"Mrs. Davis? It's Dr. Roberts. I have good news and bad news."

"Let's start with the good news."

"Okay. You're going to enjoy a measure of immortality."

"Really? How so?"

"We're naming a disease after you."

———

A patient who was having his leg amputated wakes from surgery to find the doctor standing by his bed.

"I have good news and bad news," the doctor says.

"Let's start with the bad news."

"We took off the wrong leg."

"And the good news?"

"Your other leg is getting better."

———

"I have good news and bad news."

"Let's start with the good news."

"Okay. You are definitely not a hypochondriac."

———

The hardest part about Hypochondriacs Anonymous is admitting that you don't have a problem.

A painter gets a call from the gallery that's been showing his work. The owner says, "I have good news and bad news."

"Let's start with the good news."

"A woman came in this morning and asked if I thought your work would appreciate in value after your death. When I said yes, she wrote me a check for all of your unsold paintings."

"That sounds pretty good to me. So what's the bad news?"

"She's your doctor."

———

"Mr. Jackson, your test results have come back, and I'm afraid I have a double dose of bad news."

"Just tell me. I can handle it."

"Okay. You have cancer, and you also have Alzheimer's."

"That's terrible. But at least I don't have cancer!"

Differential Diagnosis

"Hello, Mrs. Williams? This is Dr. Green at the medical testing lab. The other day, when Dr. Miller sent us your husband's blood sample, we also received blood from a different Mr. Williams, and—well, there's been a mixup and we're not certain which sample came from which patient."

"That doesn't sound good."

"I'm afraid it's not," says the doctor. "One of the samples tested positive for Alzheimer's and the other tested positive for AIDS."

"And you can't tell them apart?"

"Unfortunately, we have no way of knowing."

"Oh, my. What should I do?"

"We recommend that you take your husband into town and drop him off a few miles from home."

"And then what?"

"If he finds his way back, don't sleep with him."

Prognosis Negative

When Jonathan went to see his doctor, the doctor said, "Here's the deal: no more salt, no more red meat, and no more alcohol."

"And what about sex?"

"I'm seeing someone," said the doctor.

The Doctor Will See You Now

Old Man Sullivan was driving his doctor crazy. He called at all hours of the day and night to describe a series of extremely minor problems – some of which, the doctor believed, were entirely imaginary.

The doctor was a compassionate man, but enough was enough. "Mr. Sullivan," he said one day, "I've had it with your phone calls. I like you and I wish you well, but if you call me again with some made-up problem, you'll have to find yourself another doctor."

A week later, Sullivan fell down the stairs and broke both of his arms. He was taken to the hospital, where he was treated for his injuries. When his doctor arrived a few hours later, he looked at the patient and read his chart. Then, with a grin, he said, "Well, Mr. Sullivan, now *that's* more like it!"

The Moth

A moth flies into a doctor's office.

"What seems to be the problem?" the doctor says.

"Doc, where do I begin? I feel like my whole life has been a waste of time. I hate my job. No, I'm *revolted* by my job. But I can't quit because I'm in debt up to my eyes. And that's just the start of my problems. I no longer love my wife, and I feel guilty as hell about that. My daughter dropped out of school, and she's living with a guy I can't stand, which breaks my heart. And my son! How can I possibly love my son if he reminds me of everything I hate about myself? When I look at him I see the same disgusting, sniveling cowardice that other people see in me. If I had any resolve, I would have killed myself by now. Shall I go on?"

"You do seem to have a lot of problems," says the doctor. "But I'm a podiatrist. You should be seeing a therapist. Why did you come to *me*?"

"Your light was on."

———

This joke is sometimes attributed to the comedian Norm Macdonald, who told a much longer version on Conan O'Brien's show and claimed to have heard it from the man who drove him to the studio.

Short and Silly Doctor Jokes

What are these pills for, Doctor?
  You have walking pneumonia.
How often should I take them?
  Every two miles.

————

Doctor, will this ointment clear up my spots?
  I never make rash promises!

————

Doctor, I think I'm invisible.
  Sorry, I can't see you now.

————

Patient: Why is the doctor yelling out, "Tetanus! Measles! Rabies!"
  Nurse: He likes to call the shots.

————

Doctor: I don't like how your husband looks.
  Patient: Neither do I, but he's good to the grand-children.

————

Doctor, when I press with my finger here, it hurts. And when I press here, it hurts. And over here, it also hurts. What do you think is wrong with me?

  You have a broken finger.

————

Doctor, I think I'm a pair of curtains.

  Try to pull yourself together.

————

Doctor, I think I'm a bridge.

  Really? I wonder what's come over you.

————

Doctor, I snore so loudly that I wake myself up.

  Try sleeping in another room.

————

Doctor, everyone ignores me.

  Next, please!

————

Doctor, can you help me out?

  Certainly. Which way did you come in?

85

Doctor: The best things you can do for your health are to stop smoking, stop drinking, and stop running around with younger women.

Patient: I don't deserve the best. What's second best?

———

Doctor, I think there's something wrong with the pills you gave me last week. When I walk, I keep veering to the left and then to the right.

That's perfectly normal. Those are just side effects.

———

Doctor, I just can't get my hands to stop shaking.

Do you drink a lot?

Well, yes and no.

What do you mean?

I try, but I spill most of it.

———

Doctor, I think I'm shrinking.

You'll just have to be a little patient.

———

Doctor, I keep thinking I'm a dog.

Take a seat on the couch and we'll talk about it.

But I'm not allowed on the couch!

———

A psychiatrist was treating a kleptomaniac. He gave her something to take.

———

Doctor, I swallowed a chicken bone.
    Are you choking?
No, I'm serious!

———

Doctor, my child has swallowed a pen, what should I do?
    Use a pencil 'til I get there.

———

Doctor, I think I'm suffering from déjà vu.
    Weren't you here yesterday?

———

I'm afraid it looks serious.
    What do you mean, Doctor?
We may have to drain your bank account.

———

Psychiatrist: I think we're making good progress.
    Patient: You call this progress? When I first came to you, I was Napoleon. Now I'm a nobody.

Doctor, you look puzzled.

That's because I can't figure out exactly what's wrong with you. But I think it's the result of all the drinking.

Okay, I'll come back when you're sober.

———

Your tests have come back and you have nothing to worry about. You should live to be ninety.

But Doctor, I *am* ninety.

Well, that's it, then.

———

Patient: I keep seeing spots in front of my eyes.

Doctor: Have you seen an ophthalmologist?

Patient: No. Just spots.

———

What do they give the dentist of the year?

A little plaque.

———

Doctor, my hair keeps falling out. Can you give me anything to keep it in?

Sure. Here's a paper bag.

Doctor, I'm having trouble peeing.
　　How old are you?
I'm ninety-seven.
　　Ninety-seven? You've peed enough.

———

Doctor, I'm feeling suicidal. What can I do?
　　You can pay in advance.

———

Doctor, I've got a bad pain in my shoulder.
　　Have you ever had it before?
Yes, three years ago.
　　Well, you've got it again.

———

Doctor, I can't remember anything!
　　When did this start?
When did what start?

———

Doctor, I think I'm suffering from a serious liver disease.
　　I doubt it. If that's what you had, you'd feel no pain
　　or discomfort.
But those are exactly my symptoms!

Doctor, my husband thinks he's a goat.

   How long has this been going on?

Ever since he was a kid.

———

Doctor, those pills you gave me last month haven't been working.

   You mean the suppositories?

Yeah, whatever the hell they're called.

   Have you been taking them orally?

What do you think, I've been shoving them up my ass?

Bad Hair Day

Mrs. Cass went to the doctor and said, "I think you gave me too many of those hormone pills last week."

"Are you saying that because your voice is lower? That should go away in a few days."

"I've also noticed hair on my chest."

"Really? How far down does it go?"

"All the way to my balls."

You Must Remember This

Dr. Dropkin was a world-famous cardiologist. After finishing college in his hometown, he moved to Boston, where he went to medical school, became a doctor, and quickly rose to the top of his profession.

A few years later he was invited back to his hometown to receive an award and give a major address on the state of cardiology. Just before he began, as he was arranging his papers on the lectern, they slid to the floor. As the good doctor bent over to pick them up, he inadvertently broke wind – loudly, and right into the microphone, which amplified the sound throughout the hall.

Deeply embarrassed, he somehow regained his composure and delivered the lecture, which was very well received. Then, still mortified, he quickly left the room and vowed never to return to the place of his birth.

Many years later, when his brother was dying, Dr. Dropkin had no choice but to come back. Just to be safe, he checked into the hotel under another name.

When he arrived, the desk clerk welcomed him and said, "Mr. Green, have you ever been to our town before?"

"Actually, I grew up here. But I moved to Boston and I haven't been back for forty-five years."

"And why is that?"

"On my last visit, something very embarrassing happened to me, and I just didn't want to return."

"Well, sir," said the clerk, "I'm still in my twenties, but one thing I've learned is that the things that cause us embarrassment at the time are soon forgotten by other people."

"You may be right," said the doctor, "and I certainly hope that's the case with me."

"I'm sure it is. So this incident happened a long time ago?"

"Yes, it would have been well before you were born."

"Then I'm *sure* nobody recalls it. But let me ask you: was it before or after the Dropkin fart?"

———

This one is best known from the Broadway show (and the book, and the website) Old Jews Telling Jokes. But its origins are much older, and the joke has been traced back many centuries to a tale called "How Abu Hasan Brake Wind," which appears in some versions of The Arabian Nights.

"Getting warm . . . warmer."

LONG MARRIAGES

Our marriage works because we don't take each
other for granted. Every morning for more than
forty years I've asked my wife how she takes her
coffee. It's a small thing, but it's annoying.

—Jonathan Katz

I was married by a judge. I should have asked
for a jury.

—Groucho Marx

Studies continue to show that marriage is good for your
health, and that married people – especially men – live
longer and are generally happier than their single counterparts. No wonder so many people who have survived
a bad or unsatisfying marriage are nonetheless willing,
and even eager, to try again.

It's no secret that the last few decades have been
difficult ones for matrimony. Everyone has heard the
oft-cited and distressing statistic that 50 percent of all
marriages end in divorce, but there is reason to think
the situation is improving. It seems that the period from
the mid-1970s through the mid-1980s was an especially
turbulent time for married people, and that ever since,

the percentage of couples staying together has been gradually rising.

One reason for this is that younger people are waiting longer to tie the knot, which often leads them to make better and more mature choices. Another factor is that what used to be known as the sexual revolution has long since become the norm. "Getting married for sex," Jeff Foxworthy has said, "is like buying a 747 for the free peanuts."

It's sometimes said that the early years of a marriage are especially difficult. That may be true, but the later years present their own challenges as bodies, memories, finances, priorities, appearances, and even personalities continue to evolve. Most adults would probably say they have changed significantly over the past thirty, forty, or fifty years, and most of those changes require some adaptation from their partners.

One of the biggest pressure points in a marriage is the shock of seeing one's children grow up, finish college (or not), and leave home (or not), and some couples even agree in advance, either implicitly or directly, that they will remain together only until the kids are grown.

Of course, not everyone is willing or able to manage the many compromises than an enduring relationship requires. And a long marriage also needs a generous amount of luck. After all, there's no guarantee that even people who love each other will grow and change in compatible ways. Besides, what other commitment is expected to last for the rest of your life, especially now that people live longer than ever before?

"Have you ever considered divorce?" The question, which is sometimes asked of couples who have been together for years, often leads to the quip, "Divorce? Never. Murder? Frequently." This line has been attributed to a number of prominent figures including Jack Benny, Jessica Tandy, Joyce Brothers, and – here's a surprise – Ruth Bell Graham, the late wife of the evangelist Billy Graham. No matter who coined it, the response has remained popular because so many people have understood it all too well.

And yet there are couples who seem to glide right through a long marriage, as if staying together were the easiest and most natural thing in the world. Tolstoy famously began *Anna Karenina* with the observation that all happy families are alike, but that each unhappy family is unhappy in its own way. If the jokes in this section are any indication, all happy marriages are alike in that they're not especially funny, although in real life a relationship full of laughter is almost always a strong one.

But unhappy marriages? Now we're talking!

———

An old married couple goes to see a divorce lawyer.

"How old are you?" the lawyer asks.

"I'm ninety-seven," the husband replies.

"And you, Mrs. Green?"

"Ninety-five."

"And you've been married how long?"

"Seventy-five years."

"And you want a divorce? Why now?"

"We were waiting for the children to die."

Fair Warning

They were celebrating their golden anniversary, and in all their years together, nobody had ever heard them exchange an angry word.

To mark the occasion, the local paper sent a reporter to meet them and perhaps learn the secret of their long and peaceful partnership.

"Would you like to tell the story?" the wife said.

"Sure," said her husband. "It all dates back to our honeymoon, when we reached an understanding that still governs our life together. We were in the Grand Canyon when my wife's mule lost its footing and stumbled. 'That's once,' she said.

"We kept going, and about an hour later, her mule almost fell again. 'That's twice,' she said. Later on, when the animal stumbled for a third time, she climbed off, pulled out a gun, and shot it dead. She rode the rest of the way with me."

"You must have been shocked," said the reporter.

"I certainly was. I couldn't believe she did that. I started shouting at her and told her she was acting crazy."

"And did she agree?"

"No. She just looked at me and said, 'That's once.'"

The Easy Way Out

Four retirees in Florida were enjoying their weekly game of golf when one of them said, "I see that Christmas will be on a Sunday this year. I'd love to wake up, roll out of bed without any argument from my wife, and come here to play with you guys."

"I bet we could make that happen," said another. "Let's find a way to play at the usual time on Christmas morning."

On Christmas Day, all four men showed up.

"I'm glad we all made it," said the first man. "But what a price I had to pay! I gave Carolyn a diamond bracelet, so today I can do anything I want."

"Tell me about it," said the second man. "I told Helen that we'd go on a cruise next month, and she's home, happily looking through a stack of brochures."

"I bought Gail a new car for Christmas," said the third. "She loves it so much that she barely noticed when I left."

The fourth man said, "I can't believe how much you all spent on one golf game."

"Okay, wiseguy," said one of his friends. "How did you get here?"

"When I woke up, I said, 'Merry Christmas! So honey, what'll it be this fine morning – sex or golf?' And she said, 'It's chilly. Take a sweater.'"

The Lecture

An older man who was driving erratically was stopped by the police in the wee hours of the morning.

"It's awfully late, sir," said the officer. "Just where are you going at this time of night?"

"Actually, I'm on my way to a lecture."

"A lecture, at this hour? And what is this lecture about?"

"It's about alcohol abuse and driving after dark."

"Really? Tell me, who would be giving a lecture at this time of night?"

"That would be my wife."

The Least He Could Do

Four golfers played together every Saturday morning. But this morning was different. As they were about to tee off, a funeral procession drove by. Vince took off his hat and stood quietly until all the cars had passed. After wiping away a tear, he replaced his hat and started to line up his shot.

His pals couldn't believe their eyes. "Vince," said one, "we've been playing together for all these years, but this is the first indication we've had that you're a sentimental man."

"Well," said Vince, "after all, we were married for forty-seven years."

———

They say such nice things about people at their funerals that it makes me sad to realize that I'm going to miss mine by just a few days.

—Garrison Keillor

Redemption

Many years ago, when they were newlyweds, Donald told Sandra that he would be keeping a box under the bed. "Please promise me one thing, that you'll never look in that box."

"Okay," she said. "Even married people need a little privacy, and you can count on me."

Sandra kept that promise for a very long time. But on the day of their forty-fifth anniversary, she finally succumbed to decades of curiosity and opened the box. Inside were three empty beer bottles and close to twenty dollars in small bills and loose change.

Although Sandra was relieved that there was nothing here to worry about, she naturally wanted to know why Donald had been storing away empty bottles and cash. That night, as they celebrated their marriage at an elegant restaurant, she said, "Donny, this afternoon I broke the promise I made to you many years ago. I finally looked in the box under the bed. I hope you'll forgive me, and that you'll tell me what's so special about those three empty beer bottles."

After a long silence, Donald said, "You deserve an honest answer, although you won't like it. Every time I was with another woman I felt sad and guilty, and I'd drink a beer to console myself. I kept those empty bottles under the bed to remind myself not to make that mistake again."

"You're right," said Sandra. "I don't like it at all. But

nobody's perfect, and I guess that three infidelities in forty-five years isn't all that terrible. But what about all the money?"

"Well," said Donald, "whenever the box filled up with empties, I took them to the store and cashed them in."

The High Cost of Living

After examining her husband, the cardiologist calls Mrs. Green into his office for a private conversation.

"I'll give it to you straight," says the doctor. "He's in very bad shape. In addition to heart problems and chronic fatigue, he's showing the effects of all the stress he has suffered in recent years."

"Is he going to survive?"

"Well, that's not clear. But if you follow a strict routine, you may be able to save him."

"Of course! What should I do?"

"You can start by waking him up each morning with a big kiss. Make him a healthy breakfast and read him stories from the newspaper – but only happy ones. Be pleasant and patient and treat him kindly. Cook his favorite dinners and give him whatever he asks for. Encourage him to watch all the sports he wants on TV, even if you hate sports. Don't burden him with your own worries or with any chores. And in bed, do whatever it takes to satisfy him as often as he wants. If you can do all of this for a year or so, he stands a good chance of surviving."

As they're driving home, Mr. Green turns to his wife and says, "So what did the doctor say?"

"I'm sorry, Fred. You're gonna die."

Master of His Domain

Julian had been married a long time, and although he loved his wife, he knew she held all the power. Finally, after reading a book called *Be the Man of Your House*, he decided to lay down the law.

"From now on, things are going to be different," he told his wife. "You're going to make me a special dinner tonight, with chocolate cake for dessert. And later on, we'll go upstairs and have ourselves a little party."

"Of course, dear," said his wife. "Anything else?"

"Yes. You can draw me a bath and wash my back. And tomorrow morning, who do you think is going to dress me and comb my hair?"

"I'm thinking it'll be the funeral director."

The Imprudent Parrot

It wasn't easy to be living on a fixed income, especially when it came to buying gifts. But her husband's eightieth birthday was coming up and he had always wanted a parrot. So she went to a pet shop and asked how much it would cost to buy one.

"We have parrots starting at two hundred dollars," the clerk said, "and they go all the way up to eight hundred."

"Nothing less expensive?"

"Well, we do have one for twenty dollars, but I don't think he would make you happy."

"Why not?"

"Well, this bird comes with a lot of baggage. He used to live in a brothel, so his language can get pretty raunchy."

"That's okay," she said. "We don't mind bad language, and my husband will get a kick out of it."

She brought the parrot home and put his cage on the table. The parrot looked around and said, "Awk! New house! New madam!"

The woman just laughed. Later, when two of her friends came for tea, the parrot looked at them and said, "Awk! New madam. New whores, too! Or maybe I should say, old whores!"

The woman laughingly explained the remark to her friends and soon they were laughing, too. She was delighted with the bird's wit and couldn't wait for her husband to come home.

When he entered the house, she said, "Happy birthday, honey. Your gift is on the kitchen table."

When her husband came into the kitchen, the bird took one look at him and said, "Awk! New madam, new whores, but some old faces. Hi, there, George! How've you been?"

Promise Her Anything

Looking ahead to their fortieth wedding anniversary, her husband says, "Honey, forty years is a real achievement. I know I haven't always been easy to live with, and I'd like to get you a very special gift for staying with me all this time. What would you like? A fur coat? A Mercedes? A Caribbean cruise? Whatever it is, just tell me."

"Actually," she says, "I'd like a divorce."

"Hold on," says the husband. "I wasn't thinking of spending quite *that* much."

Confessions

As his wife lay dying, Jerry was sitting at her bedside.

"Honey," she said, "there's something I have to confess. Remember when six thousand dollars went missing from the business? I'm the one who took it."

"But —"

"I spent that money on a trip to Europe. I told you I was going with my sister, but I really went with your partner, Dave."

"But —"

"Honey, let me continue. This will help me die in peace. Remember your big tax case? I'm the one who called the IRS and told them you were cheating."

"Please, don't give it a second thought," Jerry said softly. "I know everything. That's why I poisoned you."

When I met Mr. Right I had no idea that his first name was Always.

—Rita Rudner

Serenity Now

An older driver was pulled over by a traffic cop. "Sir," said the officer, "are you aware that your wife fell out of the car about two miles back?"

"That's a relief!" the man replied. "I thought I'd gone deaf!"

———

I haven't spoken to my wife in years. I didn't want to interrupt her.
—Rodney Dangerfield

The Diagnosis

"Would you do me a favor and have a look down there?" says the man to his wife.

"I see what you mean. That doesn't look right. You may have a sexually transmitted disease."

"Ha! I should be so lucky!"

Empathy

An elderly man goes to see his pastor and says, "My wife is trying to poison me."

"That's hard to believe," says the pastor. "Are you sure about this?"

"Completely. She's feeding me a little bit of poison every day. What should I do?"

"Right now, don't do anything. In the next couple of days, I'll have a talk with your wife and let you know whether you have anything to worry about."

Two days later, the pastor calls.

"Did you speak to my wife?"

"I sure did," says the pastor. "We talked on the phone for two hours. Then she came to my office and we talked for another two hours"

"So what's your advice?"

"Take the poison."

————

I love being married. It's so great to find that one special person you want to annoy for the rest of your life.

—Rita Rudner

Upon Further Reflection

Joan and Maurice are having dinner at the club when a stunning young blonde walks in, sees Maurice, and gives him a flirtatious wave. Maurice, looking embarrassed, says nothing, but Joan sees the whole thing.

"Who was that?" she asks.

"Honey, you know I've never been a very good liar, so I'll tell you the truth. That was my mistress."

"No, seriously. Who is she?"

"I'm perfectly serious."

"Really? In that case, I'm going to file for divorce."

"Well," says Maurice, "we could get a divorce, but that would mean no more trips to Paris, no more beach house, no more private jet—shall I go on? Of course, it's up to you."

Joan, deep in thought, says nothing. A few minutes later another attractive young woman, this one a brunette, walks by and gives a friendly wave.

"Who was that?" says Joan. "Don't tell me you've got two of them!"

"No, no, nothing like that," says Maurice. "That's Carl's mistress."

After another moment of silence, Joan says, "Ours is prettier."

Since You Asked

An armed robber is fleeing the bank with a bag of cash when his ski mask falls off. At that very moment a customer comes in and sees the robber's face. The thief responds by immediately shooting the unfortunate man.

After putting his mask back on, he turns to the terrified crowd and says menacingly, "Did anyone else see my face?"

After a few seconds of silence, an elderly male voice pipes up from the back: "I think my wife caught a glimpse."

———

This one recalls Henny Youngman's famous "Take my wife—please!" Although it became his signature line, and perhaps the most famous four words in the history of American comedy, it wasn't intended to be funny. The comedian had brought his wife and her friends to a radio show. "They were all talking and giggling while I was trying to read my script," he recalled. "Finally, I couldn't take it anymore. I took Sadie by the elbow and brought her over to a stagehand. 'Take my wife,' I said to the guy. 'Please.'"

Due Diligence

An older man goes to a farmers' market for the first time. At one of the stands, he tells the vendor, "I'm here to buy some organic vegetables for my wife. Have these carrots been sprayed with poisonous chemicals?"

"No," says the farmer. "You'll have to do that yourself."

———

My mother was the worst cook ever. In school, when we traded lunches, I had to throw in an article of clothing.

—Rita Rudner

Crime and Punishment

When Herman was arrested for shoplifting, he was summoned to appear before a judge.

"What did you steal?" the judge asked.

"I don't think of it as stealing," said Herman. "I've become forgetful, and I forgot to pay."

"Well, I *do* think of it as stealing," said the judge. "What was it you stole?"

"A can of peaches," Herman replied.

"And how many peaches were in the can?"

"I believe there were six."

"In that case, I believe you will serve six days in jail."

Herman's wife stood up and said, "Your Honor, may I speak?"

"Go ahead," said the judge.

"He also stole a can of peas."

In Vino Veritas

They were sitting on the front porch enjoying a glass of wine when the woman said, "You're so wonderful! I can't imagine living without you."

Her husband smiled. "Is that you talking?" he asked. "Or is it the wine?"

"It's definitely me," she said. "But I was talking to the wine."

The Slow Food Movement

To celebrate their fiftieth anniversary, Janet was preparing an elaborate dinner for a group of their closest friends. Because she wanted to serve only the freshest foods, she sent Ed to the beach that afternoon to gather some snails to be used in the appetizer.

At the water's edge Ed struck up a conversation with a beautiful woman who invited him back to her place for a drink. One thing led to another, and Ed lost track of the time. When he finally looked at his watch, he realized with horror that he might be late for his own anniversary dinner.

He ran back home with the bucket of snails. Just before he opened the front door, he dumped them all on the front porch. When Janet heard him and opened the door, Ed looked down and called out, "Come on, guys. We're almost there!"

House Money

"I don't know how to tell you this," a man tells his wife, "but with the stock market crash, we're almost broke."

"I don't think so," she says. "Come with me and we'll drive into town."

He's too distraught to argue. When they get to town, she points and says, "See that office building? We own that. Now turn right."

Her husband says nothing. He's feeling terrible about their losses and now it seems that his wife has lost her mind. He continues driving and soon they're in the nicest part of town.

"See those three big houses? We own those."

Now he's really concerned: "What makes you think we own all this property?"

"Back when we first got married, you promised to give me a hundred dollars every time we had sex, and you always paid up. I used that money to buy real estate, and after all these years, this is what those investments have turned into. Pretty good, don't you think?"

"It's unbelievable!" he says. "If I had known you were this good with money, I would have given you *all* my business!"

How Does It Feel?

A woman is cooking eggs for her husband when he bursts into the kitchen yelling, "Careful! Be careful! Put in more butter!"

A minute later he yells, "Turn down the heat! You'll burn them. And where's the salt? You'll need salt!"

His wife turns to him and says, "What's going on here? I've been making your breakfast for almost fifty years. Don't you think I know what I'm doing?"

"Of course you do," he says. "I just wanted you to know what it feels like when I'm driving."

Pillow Talk

Bob and Cheryl Ann had been happily married for many years. One night, Cheryl Ann awoke from a nightmare and turned to her husband. "Bob, wake up!"

"What's the matter?" he asked.

"Oh, Bob, it was terrible. I dreamed that I died and you got married again."

"It's just a dream, honey. Go back to sleep."

"I can't – not yet. If I did die, is that what would happen? Would you get married again?"

"I don't think so," said Bob.

"You don't mean that."

"Well, okay, maybe you're right. I wouldn't want to live alone, and I wouldn't expect you to stay alone if something happened to me. Can we talk about this in the morning?"

"Hold on. If you got married again, would you and your new wife live in this house?"

"I have no idea. Maybe we would."

"Would you sleep in our bed?"

"Honey, how do I know? If I got married again and we lived in this house, I guess we'd sleep in this bed."

"And would your new wife use my golf clubs?"

"Definitely not," said Bob. "She's left-handed."

As You Wish

Jim and Jan, a married couple who happened to be born two days apart, are out for dinner to celebrate their sixtieth birthdays. As they're leaving the restaurant, a good fairy appears to them. "You two have been together a long time," she says, "so I'm going to grant each of you one special wish."

"How wonderful!" says Jan. "We've always talked about taking a trip around the world." The fairy waves her magic wand, and suddenly Jan is holding a stack of airline and cruise tickets.

Turning to Jim, the fairy says, "And how about you?"

"Jan," he says, "I'm sorry to disappoint you. I, too, would love to travel around the world, but I'd like to do it with a woman who's thirty years younger than I am."

"I can help you with that," says the fairy. And presto! Jim is ninety.

Just Trying to Help

A dying woman turned to her husband and asked, "Honey, have you ever cheated? It's all over now, so just tell me."

"No," he says, "I've always been faithful. How about you?"

"Well, in my case it's a little more complicated."

"What do you mean?"

"Remember when you got fired from your second job, and they took you back the very next day? I went to see your boss, and, well, you know . . ."

"Really? Well, I'm glad you did. And that was the only time?"

"No, actually, there was something else."

Her husband sighs. "Tell me. I can handle it."

"Remember when you were starting your business, and the banker refused to give you a loan, and then he changed his mind?"

"You mean to tell me . . ."

"Yes, I did it for you."

"But that was it, right?"

"Not quite. Remember when you wanted to be president of the golf club?"

"Of course!"

"And you were eleven votes short?"

Side by Side

Dave was on his deathbed. "Honey," he said to his wife, "we both know that I don't have much time left. And here you are, right by my side as always."

"That's how it is with us," she said. "I've always been there with you."

"That's true. When the business went broke, you were right there with me. When we lost the house, you were right there with me. When I lost the big tax case, you were right there with me. And when the doctor told me I was dying, you were right there then, too. Honey, you know something?"

"What's that?"

"I think you're bad luck!"

Two-timing

Two friends are having lunch. "You and Elaine have been married for quite a while," says one. "And you seem to be happy together. If you don't mind my asking, what's your secret?"

"It's very simple. Twice a week we have dinner at a nice restaurant. You know, a good meal, a glass of wine – and that seems to do the trick."

"And you do this twice a week?"

"Yes. She goes Tuesday and I go Friday."

———

Do you know what it means to come home at night to a woman who'll give you a little love, a little affection, a little tenderness? It means you're in the wrong house, that's what it means.
—Henny Youngman

Taking No Chances

They'd had a long and contentious marriage. And now, at her funeral, the pallbearers carrying the casket out of the church accidentally bumped into a pillar. When the casket was jarred, a faint moaning sound was heard from within.

The casket was immediately opened, and to everyone's shock, the woman who was about to be buried was still alive — but just barely. She recovered and lived on for six more years, which felt like an eternity to her husband.

When she died, finally and definitively, her second funeral was held in the same church. As the pallbearers carried out the casket, her husband stood up and shouted, "Watch out for the pillar!"

———

I can see my family splitting the funeral expenses like a dinner check. Okay, who ordered the mahogany inlays?
                                                      —Ronnie Shakes

One Kind Favor

Father O'Malley was greeting his parishioners after the service when a woman came up to him in tears.

"Janet, what's bothering you today?" he asked.

"Father, my husband died last night."

"Oh, that's terrible! Would you like me to conduct the funeral?"

"Please, it would mean a lot to our family."

"Tell me, did Joe have any last requests?"

"I guess he did. He said, 'Janet, please, put down the gun!'"

Reminiscing

They were lying in bed on the night of their fiftieth anniversary when she said, "Remember when we were courting and you used to hold my hand?"

Her husband reached across and grabbed her hand. He was drifting off to sleep when she said, "And remember the night you finally kissed me?"

He leaned over and tenderly gave her a kiss on the cheek.

She continued. "And a few weeks later you started to nibble on my ear?"

Her husband suddenly threw off the blanket and got out of bed.

"Where are you going?" she asked.

"To get my teeth."

Par for the Course

An old married couple are on the tenth hole when suddenly the woman collapses from a heart attack. Although he's reluctant to leave her, her husband runs off in search of a doctor.

Five minutes later he returns. "Don't worry, honey," he says. "There's a doctor back on the seventh hole, and he's on his way to help you."

"When will he get here?" she asks.

"It shouldn't be long," says her husband. "Everyone has agreed to let him play through."

The Lottery

When she heard the news, Molly drove home as fast as she could and ran into the house. "Bruce," she called to her husband of forty years. "I won the lottery! Pack your bags!"

"That's incredible," said Bruce. "But what should I pack? Beach clothes? Skiing stuff?"

"Whatever you like," she said. "Just be out of here by tonight!"

———

My friends tell me I have an intimacy problem. But they don't really know me.

—Garry Shandling

A Horse, of Course

Wilbur is quietly reading the paper when Carol walks over and smacks him on the head with a frying pan.

"Jeez, that really hurt!" he yells. "What the hell was that for?"

"When I was doing the laundry, I found a note in your shirt that said 'Rita Sue.' You'd better have a good explanation."

"Rita Sue?" says Wilbur. "Oh, sure. Remember when Benny and I went to the track? Rita Sue was one of the horses I bet on. Somebody gave me a tip, and she came close to winning."

"All right," says Carol. "I'm sorry I doubted you."

Three days later, Wilbur is watching a ballgame when Carol comes over and hits him again with the same frying pan—and this time even harder. When he recovers, he says, "Honey, what the hell was that for?"

"Your horse just called."

Simple Logic

Coming home earlier than usual from her bridge game, a woman is shocked to find her eighty-five-year-old husband in bed – *their* bed – with a much younger woman. In a rage, she picks him up and tosses him off the balcony of their fourteenth-floor apartment.

In court, the judge says, "Mrs. Rosedale, you stand here accused of murder. How do you plead?"

"Not guilty, Your Honor."

"But you threw your husband off the balcony!"

"I did, Your Honor."

"Well, you must have known that this would lead to his death."

"Not really, Your Honor. I figured that at his age, if he could fuck, he could fly."

———

I've seen this one told with a more cautious punch line: "If he could make love, he could fly." Not funny, is it? Although I prefer to avoid four-letter words, sometimes there's no choice.

Helplessly Hoping

Dave is walking along the beach when he sees a rusty old lamp in the sand. He picks it up and rubs it because – well, you never know. And sure enough, a genie comes out.

"I can't believe this is happening," Dave says. "It's just like in those stories. So do I get three wishes?"

"I'm sorry, but I'm not that kind of genie. My powers are limited, and I can grant you only one."

"Just one? That's too bad. Well, with only one wish, I guess I have no choice but to ask for peace in the Middle East."

"Ooh, that's a tough one," says the genie. "As I mentioned, my powers are limited, and there has never really been peace in that part of the world. Can you come up with something else, maybe something that's just for you?"

"Well," says the man, "there is one thing I've always wanted. In forty-two years of marriage, my wife has never been willing to give me oral sex. Can you help me with that?"

"Hmmm," says the genie, who looks visibly upset. After a long pause, he sighs and says, "Now, when you say *peace* . . ."

"Well, now that the kids have grown up and left
I guess I'll be shoving along, too."

NEW PARTNERS

I'm sure that at my funeral people will be saying,
"I didn't know he owned a suit . . . and again
without a date."

—Ronnie Shakes

Although our later years often include some pleasant
surprises, there's a reason Bette Davis famously
said that old age is no place for sissies. She might have
been referring to the fact that sooner or later, friends,
loved ones, and even spouses pass away. The survivor's
grief may lessen over time, but it never really disappears.

But life goes on and basic human instincts reemerge.

"Getting old is the second-biggest surprise of my life,"
Roger Angell observed in the *New Yorker*, "but the first, by
a mile, is our unceasing need for deep attachment and
intimate life."

Human beings have always been social creatures.
Although some people can tolerate or even enjoy large
swatches of time alone, almost nobody chooses to live
apart from other people. Even the hermits in a classic
Monty Python sketch didn't really mean it. "You know,"

one hermit tells another, "that is the trouble with living halfway up a cliff. You feel so cut off."

Social isolation isn't merely unpleasant; it's also unhealthy. Some studies suggest that loneliness can be as dangerous to your well-being as obesity, smoking, or lack of exercise. When somebody becomes mired in isolation, which is often accompanied by depression, that's a pretty deep hole to climb out of. "You have to meet new people," say their well-meaning friends. "You have to come out of your shell." While true, these comments are rarely helpful because, like depression, loneliness can be self-perpetuating.

Seeking a new partner is hard enough for younger people, but it's a whole other ballgame after forty, and even more challenging after sixty. What does it mean to be somebody's "boyfriend" or "girlfriend" when you both have grown children and maybe even adult grandchildren? Beyond the awkwardness and embarrassment, dating can be especially stressful for the woman who feels she's no longer attractive, or the man who fears he's no longer vigorous or is reluctant to drive at night.

Some of the jokes in this section depict the fumblings of men and women trying to maneuver through the tricky landscape of a new romance, while others describe the companionship of talking animals, who include several parrots and a centipede. And in a couple of old-fashioned jokes, unattached women are actually eager to meet significantly older men.

A wealthy widower of seventy-five starts showing up around town with a beautiful and much younger wife.

"How did you get her to marry you?" his friends ask.

"I lied about my age."

"You told her you were sixty?"

"No, I told her I was ninety."

Priorities

Two older men are in a supermarket when their shopping carts collide. "I'm sorry," says one. "I wasn't paying attention because I'm looking for my wife."

"So am I," says the other man. "And I'm getting worried, because I haven't been able to find her."

"Let me help you," offers the first man. "What does she look like?"

"Well, she's twenty-eight, tall, with blond hair and blue eyes. She has long legs, and she's on the busty side. What does your wife look like?"

"Never mind. Let's look for yours first."

The Prospect

A widower at a cocktail party is attracted to an elegant woman who looks to be around his age. He introduces himself and they fall into a long and animated conversation. As the party winds down, they make a dinner date for later in the week.

"You know," says the woman as they're saying goodbye, "you look a lot like my second husband."

"Really? How many times have you been married?"

"Just once."

Thank You, Please Come Again

Morris was in his eighties when his wife died. Two years later, he courted and married a kind and beautiful woman in her midtwenties. Although Morris was well off, Samantha didn't marry him for his money. She really loved him, and she admired him for being an old-fashioned gentleman who didn't even suggest that they have sex before they were married.

On their wedding night, to make sure her husband got a good night's sleep, Samantha booked a two-bedroom suite. She retired to her room but was hoping for a knock on the door. And sure enough, Morris came calling.

They soon consummated the marriage in a way that pleased both of them. Then Morris kissed her good night and returned to his room.

About an hour later, there was another knock on the door. To Samantha's surprise, Morris was back for an encore. She was happy to see him, and again, they were both more than satisfied.

She had just drifted off when Morris appeared yet again. Same interest, same happy result. But this time the astonished bride spoke up. "Honey, are you really eighty-two years old?"

"Of course. Why do you ask?"

"Because you're quite the lover, Morris. I've been with much younger men who couldn't even imagine making love more than once a night, let alone three times."

Morris looked at her in astonishment. "Wait — you mean I was here already?"

———

It's unusual to find a joke about an older man and a younger woman that's neither dirty nor cynical.

The Castaway

Mike, an avid golfer, survives a shipwreck and is stranded on a deserted island for many years. There's plenty of food growing there and the climate is mild, so he's been able to survive in good health.

One day he sees a speck on the horizon. Could it possibly be a ship? But as it gets closer, he sees that it's not a ship.

Could it be a smaller boat? But when it disappears entirely, he wonders if he has seen anything at all.

Soon he hears splashing, and out of the water steps a beautiful young woman in a blue bathing suit who is clutching a large waterproof bag. As the survivor looks on in disbelief, she walks up to him, offers her hand, and says, "Hi, I'm Karen."

"Hello, Karen," he says. "I'm Mike."

"So Mike, how long have you been on this island?"

"More years than you would believe," he says. "But I'm so glad to have company."

"Would you like a cigarette?"

"I sure would." Karen reaches into her bag and takes out a pack of cigarettes and some matches. Mike lights up and says, "I quit smoking long ago, but this is a real treat."

"I'm glad you're enjoying it," says Karen. "Would you like a drink?"

"Absolutely!" says Mike. She reaches into her bag, pulls

out a flask, and hands it to Mike, who takes a nice long swig. "Fantastic!" he says.

Then she looks at him and says, "So Mike, how long has it been since you've played around?"

"You're kidding!" he says. "Don't tell me you've got golf clubs in there!"

The Cold, Hard Truth

Mrs. Elsworth, a widow living alone, bought a parrot for companionship. But she soon discovered that a talking bird doesn't always make for good company. This one had the vocabulary of a sailor: every other word was a profanity.

When she yelled at the parrot, the parrot just yelled back. When she withheld food, the parrot's language only got worse. Finally, at her wit's end, she picked him up and shoved him into the freezer. For a few minutes the parrot squawked and screamed. And then, suddenly, the kitchen was quiet.

Mrs. Elsworth hadn't wanted to kill the bird. She only meant to scare him. Fearing that she had done him real harm, she opened the freezer and took him out.

"I owe you a big apology," said the trembling parrot. "I see now that my language was inexcusable. Being in that cold, dark place really knocked some sense into me. I had no idea how offensive my language has been. I'm so sorry!"

"I'm glad to hear that," said Mrs. Elsworth, "because you're obviously very intelligent, and it would be nice to have someone to talk to."

"I promise to change my ways," said the still-shivering parrot. "But I have to ask you: What the hell did that chicken do?"

This End Up

Dave, a widower, is vacationing at a Florida resort. Although there are plenty of single women around, they show little interest in meeting him. At the pool, he decides to ask the lifeguard for some advice.

"Let's take a look at you," the lifeguard says. "You're not a bad-looking fellow and you seem to be in pretty good shape. But your saggy old swimsuit makes you look old. Get yourself a smaller, tighter one, and a small potato, and I bet you'll get some attention very soon."

"Thanks, I'll do that. But what's the potato for?"

"Drop it into your swimsuit and it will enhance your manly physique."

Dave follows the lifeguard's advice, but the response is terrible. Now the women at the pool are actively avoiding him.

Returning to the lifeguard, he says, "I'm obviously doing something wrong."

"You certainly are, my friend. The potato goes in the *front*."

The Agony of da Feet

A lonely widower has been told by his friends that he ought to get a dog, so he goes to a pet shop to see what's available.

"Have you ever owned a dog before?" the saleswoman asks.

"No."

"Are you prepared to take it out for a walk two or three times a day?"

"I hadn't really thought of that. I just wanted a little companionship."

"That's why I asked. A dog is a lot of work. If you really want companionship, I'll show you a talking centipede for about the same price."

"You must be joking."

"No, I'm serious, and what's more, this little guy can even sing." She leads the customer to a miniature house, and in front of it, in a barely visible lawn chair, is the centipede. Turning to the tiny creature, she says, "Would you say something for this man so he'll know you can talk?"

"Okay," says the centipede in a very soft voice. "What would you like me to say?"

"That's fine," says the saleswoman. "And can you show him your singing voice?"

"Of course," says the centipede, who breaks into a barely audible rendition of "Sweet Lorraine."

The man can't believe it. He buys the centipede and the tiny house and brings them home.

Later that day, he calls out, "I'm going for a beer, and I'd love to introduce you to my friends at the bar. Would you like to come along?"

The centipede doesn't answer.

He repeats the question, and again there's no answer.

He decides to ask one more time. He goes right up to the little house and says in a loud voice, "For the last time, I'm going out for a beer! Would you like to come along?"

"I heard you the first time," says the centipede. "I'm just putting on my shoes."

The Handsome Stranger

Two widows are sitting by the pool of their retirement home when they spot a nice-looking fellow they've never seen before. "Helen," her friend says, "he looks lonely. You know how shy I am, so would you be willing to go over there and find out a little about him?"

Helen doesn't need to be asked twice. She approaches the stranger and says, "Hi, there. I'm Helen. Are you new here?"

"Yes, I just moved in," he says.

"Where were you living before?"

"Actually, I was in prison."

"May I ask why?"

"I shot my third wife."

"What about your second wife?"

"We got into a fight and she fell out the window."

"And – ?"

"My first wife? I strangled her."

"I see," says Helen. Waving to her friend on the other side of the pool, she calls out, "Yoo-hoo. He's single!"

Fool Me Once

A man and his wife are playing golf when he slices his drive so far to the side that it ends up near a deserted barn. When he finally finds the ball, he's about to take a drop when his wife says, "Wait a minute. If this barn is empty, you might be able to hit right through one door and out the other."

The barn is indeed empty, so his wife opens the back door and props open the front door. The golfer takes a mighty swing and accidentally hits her in the head, killing her instantly.

Two years later, the man and his new wife are playing the same course when the very same thing happens. Again, the ball ends up near the barn. "I have an idea," says his wife. "If the barn is empty, I'll hold the door open and you can shoot right through."

Her husband looks at her and says, "No way! Last time I tried that, I bogeyed the hole."

A Day at the Beach

Shirley, a widow, decided to take her cat to the beach. The beach was empty that day, and Shirley was reading a book, with her cat sleeping contentedly in the warm sun, when a nice-looking gentleman came over and set up his blanket not far away.

Finding him attractive, Shirley smiled and said, "Nice day, isn't it?"

"Just beautiful," the man said.

"Do you come here often?"

"I used to," said the man, "but this is my first time since my wife died."

"Do you live in the neighborhood?"

"Yes, about three blocks away. And you?"

"Not far. Say, do you like pussycats?"

Suddenly the man threw down his book, ran over to her, ripped off both of their bathing suits, and made passionate love to her right there on the beach.

When the sand had settled and Shirley had finally caught her breath, she said, "That was wonderful. But how on earth did you know that I wanted that to happen?"

"Never mind that," he said. "How did *you* know my name was Katz?"

Live a Little

A widow who was living with her daughter went on a dinner date with a man who was several years older. Later that night, when she returned to her daughter's house, it was clear from her silence that the evening hadn't gone well.

"Mom, what happened?" her daughter asked.

"He wasn't much fun," said the mother. "I had to slap his face three times."

"You mean he got fresh?"

"No, I thought he was dead."

———

To attract men, I wear a perfume called New Car Interior.
—Rita Rudner

The Impertinent Parrot

A lonely widow goes into a pet shop and approaches a colorful parrot. "Get away from me," the parrot squawks. "You're old and you're ugly, too."

The woman is angry and deeply insulted. But when she leaves the shop, she calms down. Maybe the parrot is just having a bad day.

But she can't let it go. The next day she returns to the pet shop and feels compelled to approach the parrot again.

"You're back?" the parrot says. "I told you yesterday, you're old and you're ugly, too."

This time the woman is furious. She goes to the manager and threatens to sue the store and have the parrot put down. The manager apologizes profusely. "Please, ma'am, we're very attached to that parrot, and I'm going to have a talk with him. If anything like this ever happens again, I give you my word that we will pay you five thousand dollars in damages."

The woman considers this on her way home. Is she willing to be insulted again for five thousand dollars? You bet!

The next day she goes into the pet shop again. As she approaches the parrot, he says, "Hey, lady."

"Yes?" she says expectantly.

"*You* know."

Come What May

Bernard, a widower in his mid-eighties, is about to marry a woman of twenty-three. Before the wedding, he goes to his doctor for a checkup.

"You seem to be in good health," the doctor says, "but I'm concerned about the enormous age difference between the two of you. It's more than sixty years! Please be careful. Too much sex can be dangerous, so don't overdo it."

"Doc," says Bernard, "the way I see it, we're here to enjoy ourselves. If she dies, she dies."

———

I'm eighty-three, and I feel like a twenty-year-old. Unfortunately, there's never one around.

—Milton Berle

The Virgin Bride

A woman who had buried three husbands was planning to get married again. In the bridal shop she asked to try on a white dress.

"A white dress?" said the owner. "It's none of my business, but are you sure you want a white dress for your fourth wedding? Can I show you something elegant in a pale blue?"

"No, it should be white," said the bride. "Believe it or not, I'm still a virgin."

"But you've been married three times!"

"Well, my first husband was a psychologist. He just wanted to talk about it. Then I married a gynecologist, but all he wanted to do was look at it."

"What about your third husband?"

"Fred? He was a stamp collector. And boy – do I miss him!"

————

Philatelists will point out that this one doesn't hold up logically, but jokes have their own special logic.

A common ending to this one has the shopkeeper asking, "And what about your fiancé?" The bride responds: "He's a lawyer, so I'm definitely going to get screwed."

The Mourner

Edward was putting flowers on his mother's grave when he became aware of a man a couple of rows away who was weeping with great intensity. "Why did you have to die?" the man called out. "Why, oh, why did you have to die?"

Edward walked over and said, "I'm sorry you're in such pain. I don't mean to intrude on your grief, but may I ask whose death you are mourning? Did you lose a child, perhaps? Or was it your wife?"

The mourner took a moment to collect himself. Between sobs, he said, "He was my wife's first husband."

I've been to three funerals this year, and I'm not a mourning person.

—Jonathan Katz

The Last Supper

Cynthia, a widow, is introduced to a woman at a party. When she learns that the woman was recently widowed, she expresses her condolences.

"Thank you, but in a couple of months I'm getting married again."

"Your second husband?"

"My fourth, actually."

"If you don't mind my asking, what happened to the others?"

"Well, my first husband died after eating poison mushrooms."

"That's terrible. What about your second husband?"

"Well, he, too, died from poison mushrooms."

"Oh, my! I'm almost afraid to ask about your third husband."

"Jerry? He fell off the balcony and broke his neck."

"Really? What a horrible way to die. How did that happen?"

"He wouldn't eat the mushrooms."

Speak for Yourself

On a business trip to South America, a man went into a pet shop and saw a parrot that could speak in six different languages. He bought it and had it shipped to his mother for her eightieth birthday. It was an expensive gift, but this was a special birthday for a special person. Besides, she had recently been widowed, she was lonely, and she herself spoke four languages.

When he returned home from his trip, he called her. "So, did you like the parrot?" he asked.

"I sure did," she said. "It was delicious!"

"Ma, you're kidding, right? You didn't actually eat the parrot?"

"Well, not literally."

"What does that mean?"

"I made it into soup."

"Ma, I can't believe it. That was no ordinary bird. That parrot could speak six languages!"

"Really? So why didn't he *say* something?"

Meet the Parrots

A prim and proper widow goes to see her priest. "Father, I recently bought two parrots, but they keep embarrassing me. They're both females, and all they ever say is, 'Hi, there. We're party girls. Wanna fool around?'"

Stifling a smile, the priest says, "That must be very difficult for you."

"It is, Father. I've become used to it, but it's terribly awkward when I have visitors."

"Well," says the priest, "I may be able to help you. As it happens, I also have two parrots. They're both male, they came to me as youngsters, and I've taught them to pray and read the Bible. Why don't you bring your birds over to my place tonight? Who knows? Maybe my parrots will be a positive influence."

When the widow arrives with her parrots in a cage, she's delighted to see that the priest's parrots are holding their rosary beads and appear to be deep in prayer.

When the prayers are over, she puts her female birds in with the males. The females, true to form, immediately start to talk: "Hi, there. We're party girls. Wanna fool around?"

The male birds just look at each other in stunned silence. Finally, one of them turns to his buddy and says, "Put away the beads, Matthew. Our prayers have been answered!"

The Portrait

An older woman, aware that she didn't have much time left, hired an artist to paint her portrait. At the first sitting, she said to him, "Could you paint me with a gold necklace, emerald earrings, and a diamond tiara?"

"I'd be happy to," said the artist. "Why don't you get those items and put them on?"

"I can't," said the woman. "I don't own anything like that."

"Then why do you want me to paint them?"

"Because I'm pretty sure that my husband has been seeing a younger woman. When I die, and he marries her, I want her to go crazy looking for the jewelry."

WHERE THE WILD THINGS WERE

SEX

It's been so long since I made love that I can't
even remember who gets tied up.

—Joan Rivers

You know that look women get when they want
sex? Me neither.

—Steve Martin

Can you remember yourself as a high school student?
Now try to recall how you would have reacted back
then if somebody had told you that men and women of the
age you are now were still having sex. I'm guessing that
this would not have been a pleasant idea to contemplate.

Until quite recently, even sophisticated students of
sexuality seemed to rule out the possibility that older
people might have amorous inclinations. Only 1 percent
of the women in Kinsey's famous report were over sixty,
and the proportion of men wasn't much higher. As recently as 1992, researchers for a nationwide survey of the
sexual lives of Americans didn't even interview people
over fifty-nine.

To invoke an old saying, there may be snow on the
roof, but in many cases there's still fire in the furnace.

The fire might not have any fuel left to burn, but that doesn't mean it can't be rekindled. More often than not the embers are still there, awaiting another opportunity.

And here's an astonishing fact: According to a study whose results were published in the *Archives of Sexual Behavior* and described in the *New York Times*, although sexual activity certainly declines among older people, couples who have been married for a *very* long time actually reported a slight *increase* in their sex lives, to the point where "an individual married for 50 years will have somewhat less sex than an individual married for 65 years." That's hard to believe, but what if it's true?

To be sure, some older adults have given up sex entirely, although not always by choice. And those who continue to enjoy this part of their lives typically do so with less frequency – often *far* less – than when they were younger. But in many long-term relationships, a couple's sex life doesn't stop completely unless one of the partners is ill.

Although bodily changes in both women and men are real and significant, sex, after all, extends well beyond physical performance and pleasure. Those who continue to have a sexual relationship might find that for all the physical changes they've been through, the act of love can be as emotionally satisfying, affectionate, and meaningful as it ever was. And for many others, physical and affectionate closeness may be no less rewarding.

In a rare moment of candor, a man confides to his closest friend that after all these years, sex with his wife has become routine and a little boring.

"You have to spice things up," the friend says. "You might want to try playing doctor for an hour, like we do."

"A whole hour? How do you make it last that long?"

"That's the easy part. I ask her to sit in the waiting room for fifty-five minutes."

Great Expectations

A woman says to her doctor, "I'm worried about my husband. I think he's losing his sexual potency."

"Well, that happens with age," says the doctor. "How old is he?"

"Seventy-seven."

"That's perfectly normal. As we get older, some of our functions slow down, and that's certainly true with men and sex. Tell me, when did you first notice this change?"

"Twice last night and again this morning."

———

Usually I'm on top to keep the guy from escaping.
— Lisa Lampanelli

Bragging Rites

A man goes into the confession booth. "Father," he says, "I'm eighty-two years old. I have children and grandchildren, but last night I made love to a girl who was twenty-four. And not just once, but twice!"

"Tell me," says the priest, "when was the last time you came to confession?"

"This is my first time. I'm Jewish."

"So why are you telling me?"

"Telling *you*? I'm telling everybody!"

Too Much Information

"Grandma," said the little girl, "how much do you weigh?"

"Honey, I'd tell you almost anything, but that's not a polite question to ask a grown-up – especially a lady."

"How old are you, Grandma?

"My dear, for some women, how much we weigh or how old we are – well, these things are private."

"Grandma, why did you and Grandpa get a divorce?"

"Okay, Janey, that's enough questions for today. Why don't we go into the kitchen and make some brownies?"

Later, Janey's friend told her that you can learn a lot about a person from her driver's license. So when Grandma wasn't watching, Janey looked in her purse, opened her wallet, and studied her license.

The next day she said, "Grandma, I know the answers to the questions I was asking. You are seventy-three years old and you weigh a hundred and forty pounds."

Grandma blushed. "Well, whoever told you that was right."

"And I also know why Grandpa left you."

"Oh really? And why was that?"

"Because you got an F in sex."

Easy Rider

Every home for older people has its characters, and at Avon Park, everyone knew Alice. She claimed to have been a race car driver in her younger years, and now she loved to speed around the corridors in her souped-up wheelchair. Nobody seemed to mind, and sometimes she'd get one of the men to race. Alice always won.

One afternoon she was speeding down the hallway when Crazy Carl held up his hand. Alice stopped on a dime. "What is it, Carl?"

"Have you got a license for that thing?"

"Of course I do," she said. She reached into her bag, handed him an old envelope, and continued on her way.

A few minutes later, another man held up his hand and Alice stopped. "Yes, Ted? What is it?"

"Do you have proof of insurance?"

Alice handed him a candy wrapper and said, "Here you are, Officer." Then she sped away.

A few minutes later, a third man held his hand up and motioned her to stop. He stood there completely naked, with his pecker in his hand.

Alice stopped again. "Oh no," she said. "Not another Breathalyzer test!"

Solidarity

A loyal labor leader was in Las Vegas, where he decided to visit a brothel. When the madam greeted him, he asked if she was running a union shop. She shook her head.

"Let me understand how this works. If I pay you three hundred dollars, how much does the girl receive?"

"The girl gets one hundred and the house gets the rest."

This clearly wouldn't do, so he tried another brothel. When he learned that this one, too, wasn't a union shop, he asked the madam if there were any union brothels in town.

Yes, she told him, there was one just around the corner, so he thanked her and went over there.

"I've heard this is a union house," he said.

"That's right," said the madam.

"And if I pay you three hundred dollars, how much does the girl get?"

"The house takes one hundred, and the girl gets the rest."

"That's more like it," the man said. He handed her three hundred dollars and pointed to a beautiful blonde. "I'd like to spend an hour with that girl," he said.

"I'm sure you would," said the madam. Gesturing to a woman who appeared to be in her sixties, she added, "but Allison here has seniority."

Size Doesn't Matter

An eighty-year-old woman bursts into the game room at the retirement home. She holds her fist in the air and says, "Anyone who can guess what's in my hand can have sex with me tonight."

"A loaf of bread?" says a man in the back.

"No," says the woman, "but close enough."

———

There are two ways to understand the man's guess. Either his mind is slipping or he's indicating his complete lack of interest in her offer. But there's only one way to understand her response.

A Touching Story

They fell in love in a nursing home. And every day after lunch, Jack and Serena would meet outside and walk to a secluded spot in the garden. After a few minutes, when they were sure nobody else was around, Serena would slip her hand down Jack's pants.

This went on for weeks until one day, Jack didn't show up. Fearing that something had happened to her boyfriend, Serena went looking for him. Eventually, she found him in the back of the library – with another woman. And she, too, had her hand down Jack's pants.

It took a lot to make Serena angry, but now she was livid. She marched right over to Jack and said, "I can't believe what I'm seeing!"

The other woman quickly ran off, leaving Serena to confront him in private. "Jack, I thought we had something special. Tell me – what does she have that I don't have?"

Jack blushed as he gave her the answer: "Parkinson's."

A Fair Question

"Call me old-fashioned," Harry was saying, "but I'll never get used to all these people who sleep together before they get married. I certainly didn't sleep with my wife before the wedding. How about you?"

"I have no idea," said his friend. "What was her maiden name?"

What's Your Pleasure?

A beautiful and provocatively dressed young woman shows up at the home of a widower. "I understand that today is your eightieth birthday," she says.

"That's true."

"Well, I'm here to make you happy," she says. "Your two sons thought that you might enjoy this little gift."

"A gift? What is it?"

"You really don't know? I'm here to give you super sex."

The man thinks for a minute and says, "Thank you. I'll have the soup."

———

I believe that sex is the most wonderful and beautiful thing that money can buy.

—Steve Martin

The Frog Princess

A man who was well into his eighties was fishing at the lake when he heard a faint voice calling for help. He looked around, but there was nobody in sight. Then he heard the voice again, and it seemed to be coming from a frog at the edge of the water.

He looked at the frog and said, "Excuse me, was that you talking?"

"Yes, it was," said the frog. "A long time ago, a wicked witch put a spell on me. If you pick me up and kiss me, I'll be transformed back into a beautiful princess. We can get married, and your remaining years will be happier than you ever imagined."

The fisherman considered the matter. Then he picked up the frog and put it in his pocket.

After a few minutes, the frog spoke again. "Sir, why haven't you kissed me? Didn't you hear what I told you? Don't you want to turn me back into a beautiful young woman?"

"That does sound nice," the man replied, "at least theoretically. But at my age I'd rather have a talking frog."

Catnipped

A little old lady finds an antique lamp on the beach and brings it home. On the privacy of her front porch, she rubs the lamp to see if anything will happen.

And it does! A genie comes out and says, "Thank you for freeing me. And now I will grant you the traditional three wishes."

"I can't believe this is happening," she says. "Well, to start with, I'd like to be rich."

"Sure," says the genie, who promptly hands her a huge bag filled with gold coins. "What else would you like?"

"Is it possible for me to be young again?"

"Certainly," says the genie as the old lady is instantly transformed into a beautiful young woman.

Just then, Eddy, the woman's cat, jumps into her lap, which gives her an idea. "And would it be possible to turn Eddy into a handsome prince?"

No sooner has she said the words than her request comes true.

"I'm Elaine," says the suddenly young woman to the prince, "but I guess you already know that."

"I do indeed," says the prince. "And I want to thank you for taking care of me ever since I was a kitten."

"Well, I did my best," says the woman.

"I know," says the prince. Then, as he kisses her lightly on the lips, he says, "But I bet we both regret that you had me neutered."

The Ring

On a warm Friday afternoon, a white-haired man walked into a jewelry store with a stunning woman who looked to be fifty years his junior.

"I'd like to buy a very special ring for my girlfriend," he told the jeweler.

The jeweler showed them a number of beautiful rings, but the man dismissed them all as being too ordinary.

"Give me a minute," the jeweler said. "I have something very special to show you."

He soon returned with a gorgeous emerald ring.

"Is this more like what you had in mind?" he asked. "It goes for forty thousand dollars."

"It's beautiful," said the young lady, "but it's awfully expensive."

"Don't worry about the money," the man said. "I'm going to buy this for you."

"How would you like to pay for it?" the jeweler asked.

"I'll write you a check, if that's all right."

"That's fine," said the jeweler. "But I can't give you the ring until the check clears. Call me Monday afternoon, and you can come to the store then, or on Tuesday."

"Sounds good," said the man.

On Monday, the jeweler called the customer. "Sir, I spoke to the bank and there isn't enough money in your account to cover that check."

"I know," said the man. "But what a weekend I had!"

Bells Are Ringing

When Kathy heard that her elderly grandfather had died, she went right over to comfort her grandmother.

"What happened?" asked Kathy.

"He had a heart attack this morning while we were making love."

"Grandma, at your age? Isn't that dangerous?"

"Not at all. Older people can enjoy sex, too. A few years ago we decided to limit our lovemaking to Sunday morning, when the church bells started to ring."

"Why then?" Kathy asked.

"The bells provided a nice rhythm – slow, gentle, and steady. We kept it simple – in on the *ding*, out on the *dong*."

"And you made love that way for years?"

Her grandmother wiped away a tear. "Yes, and Frank would still be with us if that damn ice cream truck hadn't come along."

Inflation

Two widowers in a retirement community decided to go out for a little fun. They took themselves to a nice restaurant for dinner, and after a few drinks they decided to visit a brothel.

"We're very busy tonight," the madam explained, "so please have a seat for a few minutes."

She then instructed the manager to prepare two rooms with an inflatable doll in each one, and said, "These guys are so old and so drunk they'll never know the difference."

A few minutes later she escorted the men to their respective rooms. Later on, as they were walking back to the retirement home, they decided to compare notes.

"That wasn't much fun," said one man. "I think the girl they gave me was dead."

"What are you talking about?"

"Well, from the time I entered the room to the time I left, she didn't say a word and didn't even move. How about yours?"

"She certainly wasn't dead, but I think she was a witch."

"A witch? What gave you that idea?"

"I was kissing her all over, but when I gave her neck a friendly little bite, she farted and flew out the window!"

A Change of Heart

An elderly single woman contacted a lawyer's office about drawing up a will. "I don't get out much," said the woman. "Do you think the lawyer would be willing to come to my house?"

"I imagine so," said his assistant. "But we would have to charge you for his travel time."

The woman agreed, and the lawyer drove to her house to discuss her estate and her will. They reviewed all her assets and agreed on a plan to distribute them. When they were almost done, the lawyer said, "The only thing left to discuss is that fifty thousand dollars in your savings account."

"Well, I've thought about that," she said. "I've lived a quiet and solitary life, and very few people have been aware of me. But when I die, I'd like to be noticed. So I've decided to allocate forty-five thousand to pay for a very elaborate funeral."

"That's a lot for a funeral," said the lawyer. "But if that's your wish, I'll write it up and I'm sure your funeral will be noticed. That still leaves five thousand unaccounted for."

"I've thought about that as well," said the woman. "I've lived alone since the age of twenty, and I'm still a virgin. But I don't want to die a virgin. I'd like to use that five thousand to pay a man to sleep with me. Will you help me find somebody?"

"Are you serious about that?"

"As you may have noticed, I'm serious about everything."

"Well, it's a very unusual request, but if you're really sure, I'll see what I can do."

At dinner that night, the lawyer told his wife about the elderly woman, her plans for a fancy funeral, and her determination not to die a virgin.

"You know," his wife said, "five thousand dollars is a lot of money, and you haven't been earning much lately. Maybe you should be the one to help her out."

"You've got to be kidding."

"I'm serious. How else could you earn so much for so little work? Give her a call. I could drive you there tomorrow, and I'll wait in the car until you're finished."

"Okay," said the lawyer with a notable lack of enthusiasm.

The next morning, the lawyer and his wife drove to the woman's house. The lawyer went in and his wife sat in the car with a book of crossword puzzles. Ninety minutes later, when he still hadn't come out, she honked the horn.

The lawyer opened the upstairs window and called down: "Honey, can you come back tomorrow? She's going to let the township bury her!"

A Word or Two

An older couple in a small town have been dating for a few months. Finally, at the urging of their friends, they decide to get married. A week before the ceremony, they go out to dinner to discuss how their marriage will work. Where will they live? How will they deal with money? How will they relate to each other's children and grandchildren?

Eventually the man brings up something that's been on his mind. "How do you feel about sex?" he asks.

"Well," she says, "I would like it infrequently."

Her fiancé is quiet for a moment. Then, with hope in his voice, he says, "Now, is that one word – or two?"

Let's Make a Deal

Bob and Marlene, both night owls, are sitting in the lobby of their retirement community after all the other residents have gone to sleep. Marlene mentions that ever since her husband died, she has been lonely.

"You know," says Bob, "I hope you won't take this the wrong way, but for five dollars I could have sex with you in that rocking chair."

Marlene looks at him and smiles, but she doesn't respond.

"Or how about this?" Bob says. "For ten dollars we could go over to that nice, soft sofa."

Marlene smiles again, but she still doesn't respond.

"Or for twenty dollars I'll take you back to my room. I'll light some candles and give you the most romantic night of passion you've ever had."

Marlene gives her biggest smile yet and starts digging around in her purse. She opens her wallet and hands Bob a twenty-dollar bill.

"Great," says Bob. "Shall we go upstairs?"

"No," says Marlene. "This is for four times in the rocker."

Recognition

Sam and Ed have been friends forever. One night, over drinks, they are talking more personally than usual. "You know," says Ed, "what I really dislike about getting older is that I can't perform sexually like I used to. I hate to say this, but I can't remember the last time Ellen and I had sex."

"Here's what I do," says Sam, "and maybe it will work for you. Right before I get into bed, I pull out my little buddy and bang it against the bedpost three times — *Bam! Bam! Bam!*"

"Doesn't that hurt?"

"Yes, but it really works."

That night, when Ed gets home, Ellen is already sleeping. Eager to try the new technique, he gets undressed and bangs his member against the bedpost — *Bam! Bam! Bam!*

Ellen stirs and says, "Sam? What are *you* doing here?"

"Good news, honey!
Dr. Bingham couldn't detect any impotence."

Doing His Part

Joyce goes to the doctor for a checkup. After a thorough examination, he says, "You're healthy, but you would benefit a lot from cardiovascular exercise. There's no reason you can't be walking at least half an hour a day. And if you had sex three or four times a week, that would really help."

Joyce blushes. "I can do the walking," she says, "but I'm embarrassed to tell my husband about the other part. He's in the waiting room. Can I bring him in and you'll tell him?"

"I'd be happy to," says the doctor.

When her husband comes in, the doctor looks at him and says, "Joyce and I have been talking about strengthening her heart. In addition to walking every day, I think she should engage in sexual activity three or four times a week."

"All right," says her husband. "Put me down for two."

———

Sex at age ninety is like trying to shoot pool with a rope.
—George Burns

Lowered Expectations

Betty was lying in bed one night when she felt her husband's hand caressing her neck in a way she hadn't experienced in quite a while. Then it slid down her side and continued its southward journey, stopping only at her knees, which was as far as he could reach. Then he moved closer and did the same on her other side before he abruptly stopped and moved away.

Aroused and delighted by this unexpected attention, Betty said, "Honey, that was wonderful. Why did you stop?"

"I found the remote."

A Helping Hand

When the farmer's truck was being repaired, he had to walk to town for supplies. His first stop was the hardware store, where he bought a bucket and a lantern. Then he went to the livestock dealer to pick up a duck and two chickens.

Without his truck, he had to figure out how to carry everything home. He ended up putting the lantern in the bucket, the duck in his other hand, and a chicken under each arm. It wasn't easy or comfortable, but he was able to manage it.

On his way home he met an older woman who asked if he knew how she could find the Robinson farm.

"I do," said the farmer. "It's just before my place, and if you'd like to walk with me, I can show you where it is."

"Is it far?" she asked.

"No more than ten or twelve minutes if we go through the woods," said the farmer. "It's much shorter that way."

"But if we go through the woods," she said, "how do I know you won't push me up against a tree and have your way with me?"

"I hope you're kidding," said the farmer. "First of all, I would never do something like that. Besides, look at me! I'm carrying a bucket, a lantern, a duck, and two chickens, so even if I wanted to, how could I possibly push you up against a tree?"

"Well, you could put the bucket over the duck and the lantern on top of the bucket, and I'll hold the chickens."

A Farewell to Arms

Marion, who was about to turn seventy-five, decided that she had been alone long enough. Stan had died four years ago, and she was not enjoying single life.

Because it was difficult to meet men, and she had never felt comfortable with the idea of online dating, she placed a classified ad in the local paper: "Husband wanted. Looking for a man in his seventies who won't beat me or run around. Must also be good in bed. Please apply in person." And she listed her address.

Two days later, the doorbell rang. When she opened the door, she saw a man in a wheelchair. The poor guy had no arms and no legs.

"I don't mean to be insensitive," she said, "but how can I possibly marry a man with no legs?"

"That's how you know I won't run around on you."

"And no arms!"

"That's how you know I won't beat you."

"And forgive me, but how could you possibly be good in bed?"

"I rang the doorbell, didn't I?"

Cowboy Boots

Jim and Jenny move to Texas for their retirement years. Jim has always wanted cowboy boots, and now that he's a Texan, he goes out and buys a pair.

When he comes home, he walks proudly into the kitchen and says, "Honey, do you notice anything different?"

"No," says Jenny, "you look the same to me."

"Just a minute," says Jim, who goes into the bedroom and removes all his clothes – everything, that is, except the boots.

He returns to the kitchen and says, "Look again. See anything different?"

"No," says Jenny. "Your ding-a-ling was hanging down yesterday, it's hanging down today, and I expect it'll be hanging down tomorrow."

"Honey, it's not *hanging*. It happens to be pointing to a brand-new pair of cowboy boots. What do you think?"

"What do I think? Next time, buy a hat!"

Full Disclosure

An older couple decides to marry. After the ceremony, as they prepare to share a bed for the first time, the man says, "There's something I haven't told you. I have a breathing problem, so you may hear me wheezing a little when we make love."

"I'm glad you let me know," says the woman. "And there's something I should tell you, too. My doctor says I have acute angina."

"Well," he says, "your doctor would know. He must have seen thousands of them."

———

There are several versions of this joke. In one, the doctor says, "You have acute angina," and the patient blushes and says, "Thank you, Doctor." In another version, she says, "Thank you. But I came here to be treated, not admired." There are also some cruder renditions that have no place in a high-class book like this one.

More than Money

Although Henry and Harriet have saved carefully for their retirement, they find themselves running short of money every month. Harriet decides that their best opportunity to earn some extra cash is if she works two or three nights a week as a prostitute.

But Henry has his doubts. "I'm an open-minded person," he tells her. "I'm as liberal as the next guy, and you still look great, honey, but is this a realistic plan at your age?"

"I've given it a lot of thought," she says. "Of course, I'll have to charge less than the other girls, but we can make it up on volume."

"I don't care for it," says Henry, "but I don't have a better plan, so let's give it a try."

They drive downtown and Henry says, "Why don't you stand in front of that bar and talk to every man who passes by. If he's interested, tell him you charge fifty dollars. If you need me, I'll be parked down the street, where I can keep an eye on you."

It doesn't take long before a potential client appears. "What's the price?" he asks.

"Fifty dollars."

"I only have twenty. Will that do?"

"I'll have to check. Wait here for a minute," says Harriet, who runs down the street to consult her husband.

"Twenty bucks?" says Henry. "That's an insult!"

"He seems nice," says Harriet.

"Why don't you offer him a hand job instead?"

Harriet runs back and explains the situation. The client agrees to the counteroffer and Harriet gets into his car. When the man unzips his pants, out pops a strikingly large and shapely schlong. Wide eyed, Harriet says, "Stay right here. I'll be back in a minute."

She runs to Henry in the car. "Is something wrong?" he asks.

"No. I was just wondering if we could lend this guy thirty bucks."

Men of the Cloth

After the death of his wife, Silverman marries a much younger woman. Although they love each other, their sex life is a disappointment – especially to her. They visit the rabbi, who offers an unusual suggestion. "I want you to hire a tall and handsome young man," he tells them. "While the two of you are making love, have him stand by the bed and wave a towel over you."

It's hardly the solution they expected, but they respect the rabbi, so they do as he advises. They hire a handsome young man to wave a towel during their lovemaking, but it doesn't help. The new Mrs. Silverman still isn't satisfied.

They go back to the rabbi and explain what happened – or rather, what didn't happen. Looking at Silverman, the rabbi says, "We have to try something else, because our tradition insists that a wife is entitled to marital satisfaction. I'd like you to bring back that same young man, but this time, you'll reverse roles. He'll get in bed with your wife, and you'll be the one waving the towel."

The Silvermans are shocked, but the rabbi has a reputation for wisdom, so they do as he says.

And sure enough, with her husband waving the towel and the younger man as her partner, Mrs. Silverman enjoys the best sex of her life, which culminates in a loud and extended cry of joy.

When the visitor has been paid and is preparing to leave, Silverman goes up to him and says, "You see, young man? Now, *that's* how you wave a towel!"

In their delightful book, <u>Plato and a Platypus Walk into a Bar:</u>
<u>Understanding Philosophy Through Jokes</u>, Thomas Cathcart
and Daniel Klein use this joke to illustrate the <u>post hoc, ergo</u>
<u>propter hoc</u> fallacy. (The Latin phrase translates as, "After
this, therefore because of this," and is sometimes referred to
simply as the <u>post hoc</u> fallacy.)

In plain English, the fact that one event follows another
does not mean that the first event caused the second, just as
the rooster's crowing at the break of dawn is not what causes
the sun to rise a moment later.

As Long as We're Here

Julie had been terribly lonely since her husband died, but she couldn't quite bring herself to go out on dates. But when Terry kept asking her out, she finally agreed to have dinner with him.

They had a wonderful time and ended up back at his place. Before long, they were in bed together.

As soon as they were done, Julie dissolved into tears.

"What's the matter?" asked Terry.

"I just feel so guilty!"

"Why?" said Terry. "We're both single, and we obviously like each other."

"I know," said Julie, "but I don't know how I can face my daughter after going to bed with you on our first date – not to mention twice in one evening."

"What do you mean, twice?" said Terry.

"Well, we're going to do it again, aren't we?"

Old Habits

They met in an assisted-living facility and it was love at first sight. A few weeks later they were married.

On their wedding night they got into bed, held hands, and fell asleep.

The next night, they again fell asleep holding hands.

On the third night, as the husband reached for his new wife's hand, she said, "Not tonight, dear. I have a headache."

Old Dog, New Trick

A boy and his grandfather are raking leaves in the yard when the boy finds an earthworm. "Grampa," the boy says, "I bet I can put that worm back in that hole."

"I don't see how," his grandfather replies. "In fact, I'll bet you five dollars that you can't get that thing back in the ground."

"I'll be right back," the boy says. He returns with a can of hair spray and sprays the worm until it's rigid. Then he puts it back into the hole without a struggle. Amazed, the older man opens his wallet and gives the boy five dollars.

"Well done," the grandfather says. "Now give me that can and I'll put it back where it belongs." Half an hour later, he comes out and hands the boy another five dollars.

"Thanks, Grandpa, but you already paid me."

"I know. This is from Grandma."

Tiers of Joy

A medical student who's considering a specialty in sexual disorders arranges to tour a clinic that treats patients with sexual problems. As the chief of medicine shows him around, they walk past a room where a man is masturbating.

"What's his situation?" asks the student.

"That gentleman suffers from seminal buildup disorder," the doctor explains. "If he doesn't ejaculate four or five times a day, he becomes very sick. He could even go into a coma."

A few minutes later, they pass a second room where a man is masturbating. "Seminal buildup disorder?" asks the student.

"That's right. About a third of our male patients have this problem."

A few minutes later they come to a room where a man is lying on a bed and receiving oral gratification from a beautiful young nurse.

"And this guy?" asks the student.

"Same condition," says the doctor. "He just has a better health plan."

"Sometimes it helps to turn a question around. Why _not_ you?"

CHARACTERS

I was a boring child. Whenever we played doctor,
the other children made me the anesthesiologist.

—Rita Rudner

As the light changed from red to green to yellow
and back to red again, I sat there thinking about
life. Was it nothing more than a bunch of honk-
ing and yelling? Sometimes it seemed that way.

—Jack Handey

One of the true rewards of growing older is a newfound
sense of freedom. After a certain age it's common
for people to express themselves more frankly, which
sometimes evokes laughter even when they aren't trying
to be funny.

It's common, too, for older adults to feel less con-
strained by other societal expectations. Those who have
always marched to their own drummer may now feel
even less inhibited, which accounts for the small and
colorful part of the older population who are known as
characters or, in some cases, eccentrics.

Oddly enough, in a world where just about every
human trait has been studied, often hundreds of times,

eccentricity has barely been looked at. One of the few researchers of unusual characters has been David Weeks, a Scottish psychiatrist and the coauthor of *Eccentrics: A Study of Sanity and Strangeness*, which was published in 1995. During a ten-year study of a thousand nonconformists in Britain and the United States, he found some surprising tendencies. Whatever their quirks, eccentrics actually suffer *less* from mental illness — especially depression — than the general population. They live slightly longer than average and visit doctors far less often. Eccentrics are healthier, Weeks suggests, because they are happier. They experience lower levels of stress because they don't feel the need to follow the crowd or to go along with conventional modes of behavior.

Eccentrics also tend to be optimistic, with an active and mischievous sense of humor. As Weeks describes it, "they themselves stressed to us time and again that humor and laughter were essential for their sense of well-being and their self-esteem in an increasingly dreary, conformist world." Moreover, their enthusiasm and their passion gives them a youthful outlook and an enduring sense of purpose.

Although eccentric types often grow more so with age, very few people suddenly become unconventional when they're older. In fact, a sudden lurch toward highly unusual behavior in a person's later years is often an indication that something is wrong, either physically or mentally.

Not all the characters in this chapter qualify as eccentrics. Some, like the man having lunch at the truck stop or the farmer with the bull, are merely exacting revenge on their tormentors. Others, like the Jewish grandmother, are showing their true spirit at a particular moment. Still others, like the farmer feeding his pigs or the man acting in *Treasure Island*, strike us as a little more extreme. And the man in this joke seems to be operating by his own special logic:

———

Two older men meet on the street. "Sam, what's keeping you busy these days?"

"I've taken up a new hobby. I'm keeping bees."

"What are you talking about? You have a small apartment and no land. Where do you keep them?"

"In the closet."

"But don't they fly out every time you open the door?"

"Well, I don't keep them loose! They're in a big suitcase."

"A suitcase? Bees can't survive in a suitcase. They'll die!"

"Okay, so they'll die. Like I said, it's just a hobby!"

Pushing Buttons

A Jewish woman who has just moved into a new apartment invites her adult grandson to dinner. "You can park on the street," she tells him on the phone. "Go to the front door, press 9-D with your elbow, and I'll buzz you in. When you get off the elevator, turn right and press the doorbell with your elbow. Can you be here at seven o'clock?"

"Sure," he says. "But why will I be pressing those buttons with my elbow?"

"What? You're coming empty-handed?"

———

My reaction to this joke has changed over the years. When I was younger, I thought the grandmother was acting entitled, that the joke was at her expense. But I now feel that by virtue of her age, if nothing else, she actually is entitled—in the original sense of the word. So she deserves a gift or two.

Just Desserts

An older man was finishing his meal at the counter of a truck stop when three large and nasty-looking bikers walked in. The first biker walked over and slapped him hard on the top of the head. The second biker, who found this highly amusing, put out his cigarette in the old man's pie. The third biker, not to be outdone, took the man's plate and turned it upside down.

During these humiliations the customer remained silent. When the bikers moved on to a nearby table, he quickly paid and got back in his truck.

When the waitress came over to take their orders, one of the bikers said derisively, "Did you see that old man at the counter?"

"I certainly did," said the waitress.

"Not much of a man, was he?" said the biker.

"Not much of a driver, either," said the waitress. "On his way out of the parking lot, he backed up over three motorcycles."

The Sting

The little old lady with the shopping bag was insistent. "I must speak with the president of the bank," she said, "or I'll take my money elsewhere."

The teller and the manager did their best to dissuade her, but she said she was about to deposit a good deal of money and the bank president would be pleased.

On the off chance that she was telling the truth, the manager brought her in to see the president.

"Exactly how much would you like to deposit?" he asked.

"There's a hundred and twenty thousand dollars in this bag," she said, holding it open so he could see that it was full of large bills. "And I have considerably more at home."

"That's an awful lot of lettuce," said the bank president. "We don't usually see cash amounts of this size, so I'm required to ask you where it came from."

"I like to gamble," she said. "I make bets."

"On sports events?"

"No, I prefer unusual bets. For example, I'm willing to bet you twenty-five thousand dollars that your balls are square."

"You can't be serious," said the bank president.

"I'm perfectly serious," said the woman. "Do you accept?"

"Let me get this straight," said the banker. "If my balls are round – or let's say, closer to round than to square – you'll pay me twenty-five thousand dollars. And if they're square, or even close to square, I'll pay you that same amount. Sure, I'll take that bet."

"Can we settle this tomorrow morning?" said the woman. "And may I bring in my lawyer as a witness?"

"Certainly," said the banker.

When the woman returned with her lawyer, she asked the bank president to drop his pants.

She took a good look and said, "Hmm. They do appear to be round. May I feel them to be sure?"

"You want to feel my balls?"

"Sir, there's a lot of money involved, and I'd like to be absolutely certain."

"Okay, if you promise to be gentle."

"I promise," she said. As she reached for the banker's private parts, the lawyer started pounding his head against the wall.

"What's the matter with him?" asked the banker.

"Yesterday, I bet him fifty thousand dollars that within twenty-four hours I'd have the bank president's balls in my hand."

The Pecker

The old bachelor farmer and his pet rooster were pretty much inseparable. One night, when the farmer tried to go to the movies with the rooster on his shoulder, he was told that animals were not allowed in the theater.

"But I bring him everywhere," said the farmer.

"Well, you're not bringing him here," said the manager.

"All right," the farmer said. "I'll leave him in the truck."

In the privacy of his truck, the farmer stuffed the rooster into the waistband of his overalls. He then returned to the theater, bought a ticket, and took a seat. Half an hour into the movie, when the rooster started squirming, the farmer quietly unzipped his fly so the bird could stick its head out and breathe more easily.

The woman seated next to him turned to her friend and whispered, "You won't believe this, but the man beside me has pulled out his you-know-what."

"Well," said her friend, "you'll just have to ignore it. There are no empty seats and besides, if you've seen one, you've seen them all."

"That's what I thought," she said. "But this one is eating my popcorn."

The Agent

A young agent from the Drug Enforcement Agency shows up at an Arizona farm. "Hey, old timer," he says to the farmer. "I'm here to inspect your property for illegally grown marijuana."

"Go right ahead," says the farmer. "But I wouldn't go into that field on your left if I were you."

The agent doesn't care for this remark. "Listen, mister, I have the authority of the federal government behind me." Reaching into his pocket, he pulls out a laminated card. "See this badge? This badge means that I can go wherever I want on your farm or anyone else's. Do you understand? Now I don't want to hear another word from you."

The farmer nods, and the agent goes off to search the property. A few minutes later, the farmer hears noise coming from the field to his left. The agent, who is running for his life, is being chased by an angry bull and is screaming for help.

The farmer saunters over to the fence and calls out, "Your badge! Show him your badge!"

The Menu

An older golfer plays a round at a new course and decides to visit the club's restaurant. As he enters, he sees a sign hanging over the bar that reads:

> Cold beer: $6.00
> Hamburger: $9.00
> Cheeseburger: $11.00
> Chicken sandwich: $11.00
> Hand job: $25.00

There are no waiters in sight, so the golfer approaches the bar and greets the bartender, who happens to be a very attractive young lady.

"Good afternoon," he says. "Are you the person who provides the hand jobs?"

"I certainly am," she says. "How may I help you?"

"Please wash your hands and make me a chicken sandwich."

The Disclosure

They had enjoyed a good life together. And now, on their fiftieth wedding anniversary, they were celebrating the occasion with their three grown children. The kids, who had been given every advantage, had all become successful, wealthy, and more than a little entitled.

Each of them showed up late for dinner, and not one brought an anniversary gift. But they did bring excuses:

"I didn't have a chance to buy you something because I've been working so hard on that big deal."

"I've been traveling all week, and I didn't have a minute."

"It's been one emergency after another at the hospital, which is why I arrived empty-handed."

"Don't worry about that," their mother said. "The important thing is that we're all together."

As the dinner ended, their father said, "Tonight I have something to tell you. As you may know, your mom and I really had to struggle in the early years. We put all of our energy into providing love and support for the three of you. Although we count today as our anniversary, the truth is that we never got around to getting married."

The kids, of course, were stunned to hear this. "What are you saying?" one of them asked. "Do you mean we're bastards?"

"You sure are," said their mother. "And cheap ones, too."

An Existential Question

A tractor salesman drove up to a farm and saw that the old farmer he had come to visit was lifting a pig up to the branch of an apple tree. As the salesman watched in astonishment, the pig bit off an apple. Then the farmer lowered the animal to the ground and picked up another pig, who also gobbled an apple. This went on for several minutes until the salesman could no longer restrain himself.

"Good morning!" he called to the farmer. "I've been watching you feed the pigs, and there's something I don't understand."

"And what is that?"

"Well, wouldn't it be easier to pick all the apples yourself and let the pigs eat them off the ground?"

"It might be," the farmer said as he hoisted up another pig. "But what's the advantage?"

"Wouldn't it save time?"

"I guess it would," said the farmer. "But what's time to a pig?"

Knitpicking

The highway patrolman noticed a very slow car in the right lane. As he pulled up beside it, he saw that the driver was an elderly woman who appeared to be knitting as she drove. He slowed down, rolled down his window, and yelled, "Pull over!"

"You're close!" she yelled back with a smile. "It's a cardigan!"

———

I've driven ten miles with the emergency brake on. That doesn't say a lot for me, but it really doesn't say a lot for the emergency brake.

—Mitch Hedberg

The Offer

Morris was retired now, but he still loved to make deals, even if they no longer amounted to anything more than saving a few cents on a grocery item.

One morning a friend approached him in the coffee shop and said, "Morris, I have a couple of pals over at the zoo, and it turns out that for three thousand dollars I can get you an African elephant."

Morris just laughed. "What am I going to do with an elephant?"

"Morris, it's not just *any* elephant. It's an African elephant — that's the good kind. Big ears, big tusks, and fierce as hell. Three thousand dollars, Morris. It's a steal."

"Let me explain something," said Morris. "I'm eighty-four years old. I live in a small apartment, just one bedroom, a living room the size of a coffin lid, and a kitchenette — not even a real kitchen. Where the hell am I going to put an elephant?"

"Morris, I'm so sure you're gonna love this elephant that I'm going to offer you an even better deal! *Two* African elephants for just five thousand dollars."

"Really? Okay, *now* you're talking!"

"Will you be passing a mailbox?"

High Standards

Mrs. Silver, a former seamstress, was walking through town when a flasher stepped forward and opened his raincoat right in front of her.

She looked at him and said, "You call that a lining?"

———

I have my standards. They may be low, but I have them.
—Bette Midler

Getting to Know You

Two older men were sitting next to each other at a bar. After a few drinks, one said, "You know, I heard you talk to the bartender and I'm guessing you'd be from Ireland."

"I am indeed," said the second man.

"And where in Ireland might you be from?"

"I'm from Dublin, I am."

"You don't say? I am as well. What school did you go to?"

"Saint Andrew's."

"Really! And when did you graduate?"

"1958."

"You don't say! I also went to Saint Andrew's and graduated the same year."

"Really! Well, the good Lord must be smiling down on us. Can you believe it, the two of us winding up in the same bar tonight? Let's have another round for our school!"

Just then another customer walked in, sat down at the other end of the bar, and ordered a beer. The bartender brought it over and said, "Eddy, I'm afraid we're in for another long night."

"You mean to say – "

"That's right. The O'Malley twins are drunk again."

An Occupational Hazard

A celebrated hypnotist was performing at the senior center. "And now, ladies and gentlemen," he said, "I'm going to put you all into a trance." Holding up a beautiful old watch on a chain, he said, "Please keep your eyes on this watch. It's a very special one, by the way, because it's been in my family for more than two hundred years."

As he spoke, he began to swing the watch slowly back and forth, back and forth. "Keep your eyes on the watch," he said again and again.

Suddenly, the watch slipped off its chain and shattered on the floor.

"Shit!" yelled the hypnotist.

It took the custodians two days to clean the room.

A Mother's Love

Three Jewish women in Miami are sitting on a bench, bragging about how much their sons love them.

"You know that Chagall painting in my living room?" says the first one. "That was a birthday gift from my Jonathan."

The second one says, "That's very nice, but did you know what my Bernie did? On my birthday he chartered a plane and brought down all my friends from Long Island for a big dinner at the Fontainebleau."

"Of course we know," says the first woman. "We were there, remember? And what about you, Sylvia?"

"I'm sure your boys treat you very well, but my Lenny is in analysis with a fancy Park Avenue psychiatrist. He goes to this doctor five days a week, and what do you think they talk about? Me!"

———

In some ways my shrink is not very perceptive. I've been in therapy for eight years, and he still thinks I'm there "for a friend."
—Ronnie Shakes

True Confessions

Four retired women are playing cards. One of them has brought along a bottle of whiskey, and after a few games the card playing gives way to conversation.

One woman says, "I need to get something off my chest. I'm a bit of a shoplifter. As often as not I'll walk out of a store with a little something in my pocket."

The second woman says, "Are we really going to confess our sins? Well, if that's what we're doing, I will admit to being a bit — well, a bit promiscuous. In the past few months I've slept with ten or eleven men — and, what the hell, a couple of women, too."

The third woman says, "Okay, I guess it's my turn. I happen to like drugs. I've been smoking marijuana almost every day since college, and whenever I can score some cocaine, I just can't resist."

The room is silent as they wait for the fourth woman to speak up. Finally, she says, "Ladies, my vice is that I love to gossip. Now, if you'll excuse me, I have some phone calls to make."

The Shakedown

A police officer on foot patrol spotted a little old lady carrying two shopping bags. It was a windy morning, and when a twenty-dollar bill flew out of one of the bags, he retrieved it and ran to catch up with her.

"Excuse me, ma'am, but this came out of your bag."

"Thank you," she said. "I really should be more careful."

Just then another bill flew out, and the policeman ran to the corner and picked it up.

"Let me help you close up that bag," he said. "Is it full of twenty-dollar bills?"

"Yes, and I'm taking them to the bank."

"Well, ma'am, it's my obligation to ask where all that money came from and whether it's rightfully yours."

"Oh, it's mine, all right. My backyard is next to a golf course, and on their way to the seventh hole, a lot of the men use my garden to relieve themselves. There's a hole in my fence, and the men treat that spot as their own private urinal."

"And you charge them twenty dollars to do that?"

"Not exactly. When I'm in the garden, I stand behind the fence with my hedge clippers. Whenever somebody sticks his pecker through that hole, I grab it and say, 'Listen up, mister. Give me twenty dollars, or I'll have to use these clippers.'"

The cop laughed. "Well, I guess everybody has to make a living. But what's in the other bag?"

"Some don't pay."

Getting to Know Me

A grizzled old cowboy walks into a bar and orders a drink. A much younger woman on the next stool looks at him and says, "Mister, are you a real cowboy?"

"Yes, ma'am, I'm as real as they come. I've spent my whole life riding horses, herding cattle, and mending fences. Yup, I'm a cowboy, all right. How about you, young lady?"

"I'm a lesbian. I spend my whole day thinking about sex with women. From the time I wake up until I go to sleep, that's the only thing on my mind."

She leaves, and a few minutes later another woman comes in and sits down at the bar. And she, too, asks, "Are you a real cowboy?"

"I always thought I was," he says. "But I just learned that I might be a lesbian."

The Method Actor

Ever since he retired, Ed has been involved in community theater. He started slowly with small parts, and now he's getting bigger roles and throwing himself into them with great enthusiasm.

One day he goes into a pet shop and asks to rent a parrot.

"We don't rent birds," the clerk says. "Why don't you buy one?"

"Because I won't need it for long. Our community theater group is putting on *Treasure Island* next week, and I'm playing the part of Long John Silver. I need a parrot to sit on my shoulder."

"Oh, you wouldn't want a real parrot for something like that. He'll poop on your shoulder, he'll squawk when other actors are talking, and it could be a disaster. What you need is a stuffed parrot. It would look real, and it wouldn't give you any trouble."

"I don't know," says Ed. "I want my performance to be as authentic as possible."

"Trust me, it'll be fine. I happen to have one at home, and you're welcome to borrow it. Can you come back on Friday?"

"Friday's not good," Ed replies. "That's when I'm having my leg cut off."

Timber!

A skinny old man shows up at a lumberjack camp. "I hear you've got a job opening," he says.

"You heard right," says the boss. "Do you know somebody?"

"I *am* somebody," the man says.

"I mean, do you know somebody for the job?"

"Trust me, I'm the guy you're looking for."

"I mean no disrespect," the boss says, "but given your age and your physique, I really don't think so."

"Let me show you what I can do," says the old man.

The boss hands him an axe and tries to suppress a smile. "Let's go outside," he says, "and you can show me your skills."

The boss points to a big, tall tree. Quick as a wink, the old man cuts it down.

"I can't believe what I just saw," says the boss. "Can you do that again?"

Without a word, the old man goes to another tree and cuts it down with a few swings.

"I'm sorry I doubted you," the boss says. "You're the best lumberjack I've ever seen. Where did you learn your trade?"

"I used to work in the Sahara Forest."

"Wait — don't you mean the Sahara Desert?"

"Sure, *now* it's a desert."

How to Get Ahead

A man with a big blue head goes to see a doctor, who takes one look at him and says, "How did *this* happen?"

"I was at the beach and I found an old lamp. A genie came out and promised to grant me three wishes. For my first wish, I asked for twenty million dollars in cash. And when I got home, I found twenty boxes on my porch with a million bucks in each one."

"Really? What was your second wish?"

"I said I'd like to meet a beautiful woman whom I could love, and who would love me, so we could enjoy the money together."

"And what happened?"

"She appeared the next morning, and we've been happy ever since."

"Really! But I'm guessing there's a little more to your story," says the doctor.

"Yes," says the man. "Then the genie asked for my third wish, and here, I think, is where I screwed up. I said I've always wanted a big blue head."

———

I've also heard this one without the last line, so it ends with "where I screwed up." I like that version, but it may be too subtle. In any case, I'm aware that absurdist humor isn't everyone's cup of tea. But this joke is a favorite of mine, and so is the next one.

Baked to Perfection

A man walks into a bakery and says, "My eightieth birthday is coming up and I'd like to order a cake."

"You've come to the right place," says the baker. "We're known far and wide for our cakes. What kind would you like?"

"How about chocolate with vanilla frosting?"

"No problem."

"And can you make the cake in the shape of the letter *B*?"

"The letter *B*?"

"Yes, *B* as in Barney."

"Well, I guess I could do that, but it will take a couple of days. And what would you like me to write on your cake?"

"'Happy Birthday Barney' will be fine."

When Barney comes back to pick up the cake, it's clear from his expression that he's disappointed.

"Is something wrong?" asks the baker.

"Yes, but it's my fault. I should have specified that the cake should be in the shape of a lowercase *B*. I'll pay for this one, of course, but can you make another cake?"

"Of course," says the baker.

Two days later, when Barney returns, the baker brings out the new cake.

"How do you like it?" he asks.

"I'm afraid it's still not right," says Barney, "but once again, it's my own darn fault. I wanted the cake to follow the shape of a lowercase *B*, and it does, but I wanted it in script, rather than print. Can you do that for me? Of course I'll pay for this one as well."

"Okay," says the baker, "but let's not go through this again. Here's a pencil and paper. Please draw the design of the cake you'd like, and if I can make it for you, I will."

"Sure," says Barney, who quickly sketches a design for the cake.

"I can make you one like that," says the baker, "but first, are you absolutely sure that everything else on this second cake is to your liking?"

"It's fine," says Barney, who pays for the second cake and leaves the shop.

Two days later he's back again, and the baker shows him the third version of the cake.

"How do you like it?" he asks.

"This is great!" says Barney. "It's exactly what I wanted."

"Excellent," says the baker with obvious relief. "Just give me a minute and I'll put it in a box."

"That's okay," says Barney. "I'll eat it here."

DEATH

If Shaw and Einstein couldn't beat death, what
chance have I got? Practically none.

—Mel Brooks

I want to die peacefully in my sleep like my father.
Not screaming and terrified like his passengers.

—Bob Monkhouse

Well, here comes the big one, which lies at the heart
of most people's fears about getting older: nobody
is all that thrilled about how the story ends. I, for one,
don't want to live forever, but I wouldn't object to a few
extra years, especially if they came during a decade of
my choosing.

Because death is such a forbidding topic, it's a rich
source of humor. Consider the many euphemisms and
circumlocutions in our language for the end of life: She
passed away. He crossed over. She departed. She breathed
her last. He met an untimely end. He gave up the ghost.
He left the building.

Some other expressions are not quite so gentle: She
croaked. He kicked the bucket. She went belly-up. He
sleeps with the fishes.

The unique and varied vocabulary of death brings to mind the memorable Monty Python sketch about the late, lamented, Norwegian Blue parrot. An irate customer, played by John Cleese, returns a parrot to the pet store when he realizes that it was dead when he bought it. When the clerk (Michael Palin) insists that the bird is merely resting, the exasperated customer sets him straight: "This parrot is no more! It has ceased to be. It's expired and gone to meet its maker. This is a late parrot. It's a stiff. Bereft of life, it rests in peace. If you hadn't nailed it to the perch, it would be pushing up the daisies. It's rung down the curtain and joined the choir invisible. This is an ex-parrot!"

As the years pass, it becomes increasingly difficult to avoid at least occasional thoughts of mortality, especially if you're arranging for a cemetery plot, drawing up a will, or simply paying more attention to the obituaries.

Fortunately, the awareness that our future is not endless can serve as a useful reminder to use our remaining time wisely. Knowing that he had only a few months left, the physician and author Oliver Sacks decided, as he put it in the *New York Times*, that he would live "in the richest, deepest, most productive way I can." His goal, he wrote, was "to deepen my friendships, to say farewell to those I love, to write more, to travel if I have the strength, to achieve new levels of understanding and insight." It's an admirable agenda, and an inspiring one.

When Diogenes, the ancient Greek philosopher, was getting on in years, he was advised to slow down and take it easy. His response: "If I were running in the stadium, should I slacken my pace when approaching the goal? Shouldn't I be running even faster?"

Some men are fond of saying that they hope to die at the age of a hundred, shot by a jealous husband. Whatever your preference, may your final exit be a good one – and may it take its sweet time in arriving.

————

Martina was concerned when her husband came home three hours late from his weekly golf game.

"Is everything all right?" she asked.

"Not really. Bob had a heart attack and died right there on the ninth hole."

"That's terrible," said Martina. "No wonder you're late. So you called an ambulance?"

"It wouldn't have helped," he said. "He died immediately. So for the rest of the afternoon, it was hit the ball, drag Bob, hit the ball, drag Bob."

The Long Goodbye

"Did you hear about Mike?"

"Yes, I heard that he died at your place. What happened?"

"He drove to our house for dinner, but his brakes failed. The poor guy flew out of his convertible and smashed through our bedroom window."

"What an awful way to die."

"No, that didn't kill him. He was lying on the bedroom floor with glass all around. As he tried to get up, he grabbed on to a heavy antique lamp, but he lost his balance and it fell on top of him."

"And that did it?"

"No, but it hurt him pretty bad. He managed to crawl to the staircase. As you know, Mike was a big guy, and very strong. As he pulled himself up, he broke off the bannister, which came crashing down into the front hallway. Mike fell, too, and one of the bannister poles went right through his arm."

"Man, what a way to go."

"Amazingly, he was still alive."

"So what finally killed him?"

"I had to shoot the poor bastard."

"You *shot* him?

"I had to! He was wrecking our house."

And When I Die

A priest, a minister, and a rabbi are having lunch and talking about their work. They often conduct funerals, and today they're discussing what they would like someone to say when their own time comes.

The priest says, "I hope somebody will say that I was a good leader of my flock and that I was faithful to the tenets of the Church."

The minister says, "I'd like someone to point out that I was a wonderful husband, a good family man, and of course, a fine leader of my congregation."

The rabbi says, "As for me, I'm hoping somebody looks down at me in the coffin and says, 'Look, he's breathing!'"

———

I hope that after I die, people will say of me, "That guy sure owed me a lot of money."

—Jack Handey

Wife After Death

A recently widowed woman was complaining to her friend about all the administrative work involved in settling her late husband's finances.

"Are the lawyers driving you crazy?" asked the friend.

"They sure are. And the paperwork is endless."

"I know what you mean. I had so much trouble winding down Tim's estate that sometimes I wish he hadn't died at all."

Crowded

Patrick and Micky were vacationing in Scotland. They were strolling through a cemetery when they came to a headstone that read, "Here lies Andrew McTavish, a gentleman and a scholar."

"Those cheap bastards," said Patrick. "Stuffing three men into a single grave!"

———

What I want at my funeral is an actual boxing referee to do a count, and at five just wave it off and say, "He's not getting up!"
                                              —Garry Shandling

Just the Facts

Mrs. O'Malley was known for her clipped tone and her emotional restraint. When her husband died, she called the local newspaper to insert a brief obituary. After offering his condolences, the clerk asked how she wanted the notice to read.

"I'd like it to say, 'O'Malley is dead.'"

"That's a little abrupt," said the clerk. "From the sound of your voice I'm guessing that you and Mr. O'Malley were married a long time."

"That's true."

"And you had children together?"

"Yes."

"And grandchildren?"

"Yes, seven grandchildren."

"Well, if you're worried about the cost, maybe you didn't realize that the first fifteen words are free."

"Really?" said the widow. "I had no idea. In that case, let's change it to 'O'Malley is dead. Boat for sale.'"

———

I hope that after I die, I turn into a fossil, because I'd like to be dusted off with one of those little brushes.

—Jack Handey

Delayed Gratification

Tony was in bed, and his energy was fading. He knew the end was near, and so did his family. But he perked up when he smelled the familiar aroma of his wife's pignoli cookies wafting up from the kitchen.

"Joseph!" he called with what little strength he had left. "Joseph, are you there?"

A moment later, his grandson appeared by the bed. "Yes, Grandpa, how can I help you?"

"Do me a favor," Tony whispered. "Grandma is in the kitchen, and I think she's just baked a batch of her wonderful pignoli cookies. Can you go downstairs and bring me a couple?"

A minute later the boy returned empty-handed and said, "Sorry. She says they're for later."

———

The Jewish version ends with, "She says they're for the shiva."
Another option: "She's saving them for the wake."

Recognition

Lou Schwartz died after a brief illness. When the mortician prepared the body, he was astonished by the size of Mr. Schwartz's phallus. He had been in the funeral business all his life, and this was the most prodigious penis he had ever seen.

It was so large, the mortician decided, and so magnificent, that a record of it had to be saved for posterity. Although he had never done anything like this before, he photographed the deceased's naked body – but only from the waist down, so as not to violate Mr. Schwartz's privacy.

When he got home, he said to his wife, "Honey, this is completely unprofessional, but I'm going to show you something you just won't believe."

His wife took one look at the photograph and screamed, "Oh my God! Schwartz is dead!"

A Happy Ending

One afternoon, Mrs. McRory answered the door and found her husband's best friend standing there.

"Good day, Paddy," she said. "But where's my Brian? I thought he went with you to tour the beer factory."

"He did. He did indeed. But there was a terrible accident. Your poor husband fell into a vat of Guinness and drowned."

Mrs. McRory burst into tears. "I can't believe it," she cried. When she was able to speak, she asked, "Did he at least go quickly?"

"Not really," said Paddy. "He climbed out three times to pee."

Longevity

Three Irishmen leave a pub on a moonlit night and start walking home on a road that takes them through the local cemetery.

"Have a look at this," says the first man. "It's Mike O'Donnell's grave. Remember Mike? It says here that he lived to be eighty-nine. What a fortunate man."

"And look over here," says the second man. "It's Pat O'Grady's grave. He lived to be ninety-two. Another fortunate fellow."

"That's nothing," says the third man. "Here's someone who lived to be a hundred and twenty-five."

"I can't believe it," says the first man. "What was his name?"

"Miles."

"Miles what?"

"Wait—let me see. There it is: Miles to Dublin."

———

You know when you're getting old, there are certain signs. I walked past a cemetery and two guys ran after me with shovels.
—Rodney Dangerfield

Take a Number

Anne is walking down the street when she notices an unusual funeral procession. Two hearses are moving slowly, and behind them, on foot, is a woman dressed in black. And behind her about forty other women, all of a certain age, are walking in single file.

Anne runs up to the woman in black and says, "I'm sorry for intruding on your grief, but whose funeral is this?"

"It's my husband's. He was killed by my dog, who tracked him down and found him with his girlfriend."

"And what about the second hearse?"

"The dog killed the girlfriend as well."

"Really? Could I possibly borrow your dog?"

"Sure," says the widow. "But you'll have to get in line."

———

In another version of this joke, the mourner is a man whose dog has killed both his wife and his mother-in-law.

So Little Time

"Doctor, I'm feeling terrible."

"Okay, let's have a look."

A few minutes later, the doctor says, "I'm afraid you're dying and you don't have much time."

"Well, how long do I have?"

"Ten."

"Ten what? Months? Weeks?"

"Nine."

"Nine *what*?"

"Eight . . . Seven . . ."

Surprise Ending

The woman was in tears when she came to the rabbi.

"Esther, I can see that you're grieving. How can I help you?"

"Rabbi, my dog died yesterday, and it would mean so much to me if you would do the funeral."

"I'm terribly sorry," the rabbi said, "but I can only hold a funeral service for a person."

"Please, Rabbi," she said. "I'm alone in the world and Cooper meant everything to me. I'm also prepared to make a substantial donation to the synagogue."

The rabbi held firm for a while, but in the end he was overwhelmed by the woman's tears, her obvious love for the dog, and also, perhaps, by her pledge to help the synagogue. So the next day he held a small funeral service in her backyard and gave a beautiful eulogy.

When it was over, Esther said, "Rabbi, that was everything I was hoping for. It was so moving! I thought I knew everything about Cooper, but honestly, I had no idea how much he had done for Israel!"

The Old Switcheroo

Virginia was heartbroken when her husband died. The next day she dragged herself to the funeral home to have one last look at the man she had loved all these years. When she burst into tears at the sight of him, the funeral director approached her to offer some comfort.

"This is just wrong!" she said.

"I know," he said. "Who can fathom the ways of God?"

"No, not that," said Virginia. "It's wrong that he's wearing a black suit."

"But that's how we always do it."

"He specifically told me that he wanted to be buried in a blue suit."

"Really?" the funeral director said. "Well, the ceremony isn't until tomorrow, which may give us enough time to get it right."

When Virginia returned the next day, the funeral director pulled back the curtain to reveal that her late husband was now wearing a blue suit – and a beautiful one, too.

"Thank you," she said. "But where did you get that elegant blue suit? And how much do I owe you for it?"

"There's no charge. Yesterday, a couple of hours after you left, a man was brought in who was wearing a nice blue suit. As it happened, his wife wanted him to be buried in the traditional black suit."

"Aha," said Virginia. "So all you had to do was – "

"That's right. We just switched the heads."

Have a Heart

Ethel goes to the doctor for her annual checkup. After the exam, he shakes his head sadly and explains that she has only a few hours to live.

She drives home and tells her husband the sad news. "Honey," she says, "if this is our last night together, I'd like to spend it in a romantic way."

"Of course," says her husband. "Whatever you like."

They go out for a wonderful dinner, and when they come home, they make love. An hour later, Ethel says, "That was wonderful, dear. Can we do it again?"

"I don't know if I can manage it a second time," he says.

"It's my final wish," she says.

He makes a supreme effort, and Ethel is both pleased and grateful.

At 3:00 a.m. she wakes him up and says, "Just once more, okay?"

"Give me a break," he says. "Some of us have to get up in the morning."

This Way Out

A man is discussing funeral arrangements with his elderly mother.

"I hate to bring this up," he says, "but would you rather be buried or cremated?"

"I don't know," she says. "Surprise me."

———

My aunt died last week. She was cremated. We think that's what did it.

—Jonathan Katz

The Convert

A pious Jew is near death when his wife asks if he has any final requests.

"Just one," he says. "Can you bring in a Catholic priest so I can convert?"

"Are you crazy?" she says. "You've devoted your whole life to prayer, study, and charity. Why on earth do you want to convert?"

"Well, the way I see it, better one of them should die than one of us."

———

Not surprisingly, this joke exists in another version:

It was a cold and stormy night and Sean Kennedy knew he was dying.

"The end is near," he told his wife. "Please call a rabbi."

"Why a rabbi? You're a devout Catholic!"

"That's true. But I'd hate to ask a priest to come out on a night like this."

Anticipation

A little boy ran up to his grandfather to ask if he could talk like a frog.

"No, I don't think I can," said the grandfather.

A minute later, his granddaughter came to him with the same question.

"No, I really don't know how."

"Do you think you could learn?" she asked.

"I guess so. But why are you both asking me this?"

The little girl looked up at him and said, "We heard Daddy tell Mommy that when you croak, we can all go to Disneyland."

———

I don't want to live on in the hearts of my countrymen. I want to live on in my apartment.

—Woody Allen

Theory of Relativity

The congregational rabbi was on vacation, so a substitute was conducting the funeral. "My friends," he said, "we are gathered here to honor the memory of Sam Goldberger, a good and honest man."

"Rabbi," somebody called out, "are you serious? Goldberger would cheat his own grandmother!"

"I'm sorry. Let me start again. We are here to honor the memory of our dear friend, a pillar of the synagogue."

"Not true!" another mourner called out. "We never saw him here."

The rabbi paused and began again: "We are here to mourn the passing of our dear friend, Mr. Goldberger, a loving husband and a dedicated father."

"Don't make me laugh!" somebody yelled. "He was a terrible husband and a cruel father who used to beat his children."

The rabbi was silent for a moment. "Dear friends," he said, "it must be obvious by now that I didn't know the deceased. Is there anyone here with a good word to say about Mr. Goldberger?"

After a long silence, an old man in the back stood up and said, "His brother was worse."

Heroic Measures

Mrs. Wilson had been in a coma for weeks. But one morning, the nurse who was giving her a sponge bath noticed a flicker of life on the monitor. She had been washing the patient's private parts, and when she touched that same spot a few minutes later, the monitor again showed a slight response.

The nurse quickly reported this hopeful sign to the doctor, who immediately called Mrs. Wilson's husband. "I can't believe I'm saying this," the doctor said, "but nothing else has worked. Why don't you come to the hospital and see her? It's a long shot, but it's possible that a little oral sex could bring her out of the coma."

"I'll be right over," the husband said.

Shortly after Mr. Wilson arrived, he ran into the hall in great distress, calling loudly for help.

Two nurses came running into Mrs. Wilson's room, but it was too late. The poor woman was dead.

"What happened?" they asked her husband.

"I'm not sure," he said. "I think she choked."

———

Too crass? You should see the ones I left out.

Sure Shot

Two old friends are hunting in the woods when one of them suddenly collapses. He doesn't seem to be breathing and his eyes are glazed over. His companion takes out his cell phone and calls 911. "I think my friend is dead," he says. "What should I do?"

"Stay calm," says the operator. "I'm going to help you through this. First, let's make sure he's really dead."

"Okay, hold on," says the caller. There is a silence, followed by the sound of a gunshot.

"Okay," says the hunter. "He's really dead. Now what?"

———

True story: A research project conducted in 2002 by a professor at the University of Hertfordshire surveyed people in a number of countries and concluded that this was "the world's funniest joke."

But you'll be the judge of that.

A Battle of Wills

As Max lay dying, he called his wife to his bedside and said, "You know, I always meant to draw up a will, but I never got around to it. So please pay close attention to my final wishes."

"Of course," she said through her tears. "Whatever you want, I'll make sure it happens."

"First, I'm leaving the business to Joey."

"No, Max! Not Joey. He'll ruin it. Leave the business to Jerome. He's a real businessman."

"Okay, Jerome. Let Joey have my stock portfolio."

"That's a bad idea, Max. He'll just spend the money on girls and booze. Better to leave the portfolio to me."

"Okay, then. And the summer house goes to Marion."

"Marion hates the water. She'll never use that place. How about Amy?"

"Okay, the summer house goes to Amy. And I'd like the paintings to go to Alan."

"Alan has no appreciation for art. Give the paintings to your nephew, Steve."

Max had heard enough. Lifting himself off the pillow, he said, "Honey, who's dying around here – you or me?"

"I'd like to go back and change my shirt."

THE AFTERLIFE

I don't believe in an afterlife. I don't even believe in *this* life.

—Fran Lebowitz

If there is a Hell, it is modeled after junior high school.

—Lewis Black

Throughout recorded history, the most enduring response to the mystery of death has been the hopeful idea that some dimension of human life extends beyond the grave. Most religious traditions include a version of an afterlife, and the popular American beliefs about Heaven and Hell come from early post-biblical Christianity. The Hebrew Bible says almost nothing about a life after this one, and the New Testament includes little about Heaven and even less about Hell.

Historically, Heaven has been portrayed by Christian authorities as a shining celestial city, and Hell as a place where unfortunate sinners suffer unspeakable torments. But in recent years the idea of Hell seems to be fading. In liberal and mainline churches there is little talk of Heaven and virtually none about that other place. And yet in one poll after another, a majority of American adults say they believe in both.

Many jokes about the afterlife feature Saint Peter, who is portrayed as the gatekeeper of that paradisiacal property where everyone hopes to end up. His unique assignment was extrapolated long ago from a verse in Matthew where Jesus says to Peter, "I will give you the keys of the kingdom of Heaven." This was almost certainly meant as a figure of speech, as there is nothing in Scripture to suggest that people who have just died arrive at a celestial portal where an admissions officer decides whether to admit them or send them elsewhere.

In *Life After Death: A History of the Afterlife in Western Religion*, Alan F. Segal outlines some of the common beliefs that comprise the standard American view of Heaven. Among other things, it's a realm where angels dwell, the crippled will be healed, the inhabitants will be recognizable, and they will live forever in a world without sickness or pain, troubles or sorrow.

Hell, of course, is a very different story. The Hebrew Bible includes references to Sheol, a shadowy place beneath us where human souls are separated from God after death, regardless of their moral conduct while they were alive. When the Old Testament was translated into Greek, Sheol became Hades, which refers to the Greek underworld. As Christianity grew over the centuries, the idea of Hell was further embellished and its torments grew more elaborate.

But as early as the second century, a Christian text known as Apocalypse of Peter provided elaborate visions of both Heaven, where people wore shiny clothes and sang in celestial choirs, and Hell, which featured hideous punishments that were deemed appropriate for particular sins.

Most jokes about the Afterlife are set in Heaven, although in other sections of this book the jokes are more likely to describe negative outcomes. Could this mean that Hell is just too frightening a subject to joke about? Or does Heaven simply provide better opportunities for laughter?

Another thing that surprised me is that in the world of jokes, even outright sinners make no attempt to lie to Saint Peter about their earthly conduct. If they're destined for Hell in any case, what have they got to lose by fudging the truth and trying to arrange for a better future?

———

Howard was a good and honest man, and when he arrived at the Gates of Heaven, he had no need to lie. He was soon directed to the men's entrance, where he found two smaller gates. The first one had a sign that read "For Men Who Were Dominated by Their Wives," while the second was marked "For Men Who Headed Their Households."

Howard wasn't sure which line to join. But it took only a moment to see that the line in front of the first gate seemed to stretch forever, while the second line, for men who headed their households, had only one person. So Howard joined the second line and tapped the other man on the shoulder. "Excuse me," he said, "but I'm wondering why you're the only one in this line."

"I'm not sure," the man replied. "My wife told me to stand here."

The Entrance Exam

A woman arrived at the Pearly Gates. "Did I really make it to Heaven?" she asked.

"You certainly did," said Saint Peter. "You've lived a righteous life, so all you have to do to be admitted is to spell one word."

"Okay," she said with a smile, for she had always been a good speller. "What's the word?"

"The word is *love*."

A moment later, Saint Peter welcomed her in.

Three years later, Saint Peter asked her to fill in for a few hours as the Heavenly Gatekeeper. As it happened, among that day's new arrivals was her widowed husband.

"Tom, you're finally here! How have you been?"

"Terrific! Remember that pretty young nurse who took care of you in your final months? Well, I married her. Then, of all things, I won the lottery! We bought a big new house and traveled all around the world. I've never been happier — until today, when I was hit by a car and ended up here."

"Well, in order to be admitted, you'll have to spell a word."

"Sure. What it is?"

"Chrysanthemum."

Reversal of Fortune

It was a crazy coincidence when President Bill Clinton and the Pope died on the very same day, and it caused some confusion upstairs. Due to an administrative error, the president was sent to Heaven and the Pope ended up in Hell.

When the mistake was discovered, Saint Peter and the Devil conferred on their special hotline. But there are bureaucracies even in the Afterlife, and it took a day or so before everything was straightened out.

On his way up to Heaven on a secret and rarely used staircase, the Pope met President Clinton, who was traveling in the other direction.

"I'm sorry about the mixup," said the Pope.

"Not as sorry as I am," said the president.

"I have to tell you, I'm really excited about going to Heaven," said the Pope.

"Is there anyone in particular you're hoping to meet?"

"Well, I've always wanted to kneel at the feet of the Virgin Mary."

"I don't quite know how to tell you this," said the president, "but I'm afraid you're a day late."

The No Good, Very Bad Day

Some say it was due to temporary overcrowding, while others insist that the gatekeeper just wanted to try something different. But they all agree that for a few hours, Saint Peter had quietly decided to admit only people whose final hour on earth had been especially unpleasant.

"Tell me about your day," he said to the first man in line.

"It was terrible," he replied. "I thought my wife might be having an affair, so I came home earlier than usual. She was dressed provocatively and acting funny, but I couldn't find the guy anywhere. Finally, I looked on the balcony, where I found him hanging over the edge. We live on the twentieth floor, but I was so angry that I got a hammer and started pounding his fingers. He held on for a while, but eventually he let go and fell into some bushes. But he was still alive, and I somehow found the strength to carry out the refrigerator and drop it on him. That finished him off. But it also finished me off. I had a heart attack and – well, here I am."

Saint Peter didn't hesitate to admit him. This guy had certainly had a bad day.

He then asked the second man to describe his day.

"Worst day of my life," he said. "We live on the twenty-second floor, and I was exercising on the balcony when I somehow fell over the edge. Fortunately, I managed to grab on to the balcony two floors down. I was hanging on by my fingertips when this maniac comes out and starts pounding on my fingers with a hammer. When I finally

258

let go, I was lucky enough to fall into some bushes, and believe me, I was grateful to be alive. But then something even crazier happened. A refrigerator fell on me, and that was the end."

Saint Peter admitted him and turned to the third man.

"How was my day?" he said. "Really strange – and painful, too! Last thing I remember, I was in my underwear, hiding in a fridge . . ."

She Gets Around

Three men arrive together at the Gates of Heaven. Saint Peter greets the first man and says, "I have only one question. Were you faithful to your wife?"

"Yes, completely. I barely even looked at another woman."

Saint Peter hands him some car keys and says, "See that Rolls-Royce? That will be your car in Heaven."

Responding to the same question, the second man says, "I was faithful, but not one hundred percent. During our marriage I slipped up twice."

Saint Peter hands him the keys to a new Toyota Camry.

The third man answers a little sheepishly: "I'd like to think of myself as a good person, but I had a real weakness when it came to women."

"I know that, of course," says Saint Peter. "And because in other ways you really were a good man, you will still be admitted. All I can give you is a bicycle, but it works fine and you'll be able to get around."

A few weeks later, the second and third men are driving together in the Camry when they see the first man's Rolls-Royce parked outside a bar. They go inside and find him sitting morosely, surrounded by empty bottles.

The second man says, "Bob, what's the matter? Here you are in Heaven and you're driving a Rolls-Royce. Why are you sad?"

"I just saw my wife."

"What's the problem? You loved your wife."

"I sure did. But she was riding a skateboard."

A Movable Feast

A cat arrives at the Pearly Gates. "Wow," he says to Saint Peter. "I never expected to get to Heaven."

"It's a little unusual," says Saint Peter, "but an animal who is exceptionally kind on earth will sometimes end up here. Is there anything you've always wanted that we can provide for you?"

"Well," says the cat, "my master used to have a soft satin pillow, and I've always wanted to lie on one just like it."

"We can do that," says Saint Peter. "Go in through that gate and your pillow will be waiting."

A few minutes later a group of mice appears, and they, too, are surprised to be in Heaven. Saint Peter explains that they were especially well behaved on earth and asks if there's anything they've always wanted.

"Actually, yes," says the head mouse. "We used to watch children roller skating, and it looked like so much fun. Would it be possible for us to have roller skates in Heaven?"

"Absolutely," says Saint Peter. "You'll receive them within the hour."

A couple of days later, Saint Peter is strolling through Heaven when he sees the cat. "Are you enjoying your satin pillow?" he asks.

"I am," says the cat. "Thank you for providing it. And that Meals on Wheels program is a *very* nice touch."

To Each His Own

A woman arrives at the Pearly Gates and is greeted by Saint Peter. "Welcome to Heaven," he says. "Your placement here depends on your religious affiliation. Are you a Christian?"

"Yes, I am."

"What denomination?"

"Methodist."

"In that case," says Saint Peter, "please report to room 312 to register. But be very quiet as you pass room 304."

"Okay," she says, "but why is that?"

"That's where the Baptists register, and they think they're the only ones here."

———

Naturally, the identical joke is told about most other denominations.

That's What She Said

When three nuns die in a car accident, Saint Peter greets them at the Pearly Gates. "I'm sure you have all led virtuous lives," he says, "but everyone admitted to Heaven must first answer a question."

"Nobody told us about this part," says one of the nuns.

"Don't worry, it's pretty much a formality. Most of the questions are very easy, although there can be a few surprises."

Turning to the first nun, Saint Peter says, "Can you tell me the name of the first man God created?"

"That would be Adam," she answers. Immediately, a heavenly choir responds with a loud and resplendent "Hallelujah" and the Pearly Gates open just for her.

Turning to the second nun, Saint Peter says, "Can you tell me the name of the first woman God created?"

"That would be Eve," she says. Again the choir sings "Hallelujah" and the Heavenly Gates open.

As he turns to the third nun, Saint Peter looks at his notebook and says, "I'm afraid your question is a little more challenging. What was the first thing that Eve said to Adam?"

"Oh, my," says the nun. "That really is a hard one."

Whereupon the choir again sings "Hallelujah" and the Pearly Gates open once more.

A Curve Ball

Barry and Earl were old friends who knew each other from their college baseball team. Barry was a pitcher, Earl was his catcher, and they were a terrific twosome. Neither one made it to the pros, but over the next sixty years they went to games together and talked about baseball almost every day, either on the phone or over lunch. As they grew older, they sometimes joked that whoever died first would somehow find a way to inform the other whether, as they fervently hoped, there was baseball in Heaven.

One night, Earl died peacefully in his sleep. A couple of weeks later, Barry awoke and heard his friend's voice calling his name as clearly as if he were in the room.

"Earl, is that really you?" he asked.

"Of course!" said the voice. "We had a deal, remember?"

"So what's the story? Is there baseball in Heaven?"

"Is there ever! We play every day!"

"I'm so glad to hear that!"

"Yes, but there's a little more to it."

"How so?"

"I checked the schedule. You're pitching Sunday."

Presumed Guilty

After a terrible earthquake struck the hotel during a convention of priests, fifty clergymen arrived together at the Pearly Gates.

"I'll get right to the point," said Saint Peter. "How many of you have acted inappropriately with boys?"

Forty-nine hands shot up.

"That's what I thought," said Saint Peter. "All forty-nine of you are going to Hell. Oh – and take that deaf guy with you."

Why a Duck?

When three women arrive in Heaven at the same time, Saint Peter welcomes them and says, "Ladies, we have only one rule here. Whatever you do, don't step on a duck."

There are ducks everywhere – so many that it's very difficult to avoid them. Within a few minutes, one of the women steps on a duck.

Saint Peter appears a moment later with an extremely ugly man. "I'm so sorry," he says, "but your punishment for stepping on a duck is to spend the next year chained to this man."

"A whole year?" she says.

"You're very fortunate. Until a few years ago, the penalty for stepping on a duck went on for all of eternity."

The next day, the second woman steps on a duck. And again Saint Peter appears with a very ugly man and chains them together for a year.

The third woman is exceedingly careful and avoids stepping on any ducks. On her third day in Heaven, Saint Peter appears, accompanied by a strikingly handsome man. The woman is so relieved that she falls to her knees and says, "Thank you, Lord, although I don't know what I have done to deserve this."

"Neither do I," says the man. "All I did was step on a duck."

Time Flies

A virtuous man arrives in Heaven and meets Saint Peter, who quickly admits him. It's a slow day, so Saint Peter decides to give him a tour of the place. As they walk down the halls, there are clocks everywhere, and they all seem to be running at different speeds.

"Saint Peter," he says, "I hope you don't mind my asking, but what are all these clocks for? And why do they all show a different time?"

"Oh, these aren't for telling time. We have a clock here for every person on earth, and each time they commit a sin, their clock ticks."

Soon they pass a clock that seems to be lagging well behind all the others. "Whose clock is that?" the man asks.

"That one is for the Pope," says Saint Peter. "He's an unusually righteous man. Come with me, and I'll show you the clocks that keep track of other well-known people."

When the tour is over, the new arrival says, "As a political junkie, I must ask you about a clock that I didn't see. Where's the one for Bill Clinton?"

Saint Peter chuckles. "That one is special," he says. "We keep it in the office and use it as a fan."

The Sidekick

An unusually righteous man dies and goes to Heaven. As a reward for his exemplary life, Saint Peter gives him a rare VIP tour, which includes a brief glimpse of God. And sitting next to God is a man with a mop and a bucket who appears to be a janitor.

The new arrival is too intimidated to speak, but when the tour is over, he turns to Saint Peter and says, "Tell me, who was that fellow sitting next to God?"

"That," says Saint Peter, "was Cleanliness."

———————

People say, "She's in a better place." How do we know it's a better place? You know what's a better place? Maui.

—Dom Irrera

"You'll be in charge of the music down here."

Nobody's Perfect

Three nuns arrive together at the Heavenly Gates.

"You must be without sin to enter," says Saint Peter. "But because nobody is perfect, you may confess your sins and wash them away in this basin of holy water."

"I once saw a man's penis," says the first nun. "Was that a sin?"

"Nobody's perfect," says Saint Peter. "Just wash your eyes and enter."

"And I touched a man's penis," says the second nun.

"You are forgiven," says Saint Peter. "Just put your hands in the holy water."

Suddenly the fourth nun pushes ahead and plunges her face into the basin.

"Sister, please!" says Saint Peter. "Can you wait your turn?"

"Not today," she replies. "If I'm going to gargle, I'd like to do it before Sister Margaret dips her ass in there."

Turn, Turn, Turn

Donna really missed her husband, who had died several years earlier. When she arrived at the Pearly Gates, she immediately asked Saint Peter for help in finding him.

"Of course," Saint Peter said. "What's his name?"

"Patrick Miller."

"Patrick Miller? We have many men with that name. Can you tell me something specific about him?"

"Well, the last thing he said before he died was that if I ever went out with another man, he would turn over in his grave."

Saint Peter smiled. Turning to his assistant, he said, "Where, exactly, would we find Pinwheel Pat?"

What's Not to Like?

Arthur dies and is shocked to end up in Hell. He's devastated, so the Devil tries to cheer him up. "Why the long face?" he asks.

"Are you kidding?" he says. "I'm in Hell, aren't I?"

"What do you know about Hell?" says the Devil. "Nothing you've heard about this place is true. We actually have a great time here."

"Oh yeah?" says Arthur. "Like what?"

"Well, do you like to drink?"

"Do I like to drink? I *love* to drink. Are you telling me there's booze here?"

"Of course there is. On Monday, drinking is pretty much all we do. Whether it's whiskey, tequila, bourbon or beer, wine – you name it, we've got it. We all get drunk and nobody gets a hangover."

"Really? Why not?"

"Because you're already dead, right?"

"I never thought of it that way."

"So that's Monday. Do you like smoking?"

"Sure. I used to smoke, but I gave it up for health reasons."

"Well, if it's cancer you're worried about, you're already dead, right? Every Tuesday we pass around cigarettes and cigars from all over the world. You can smoke your brains out. Hey, do you like to gamble?"

"Sure. Are you telling me that Wednesday is Casino Day?"

"You guessed it!" says the Devil. "You can gamble to your heart's content. We have everything from bingo to baccarat, blackjack, poker, roulette, slots — whatever you like. And if you lose all your money — "

"Let me guess. It doesn't matter because you're dead anyway!"

"Exactly. And Thursday is Drug Day. You like drugs?"

"I sure do!"

"We've got everything from aspirin to opiates, hash to heroin, along with crack, coke, and pills of every kind and color."

"I can't believe this. I never realized that Hell was such a cool place!"

"But wait — there's more! Are you gay?"

"No. Why do you ask?"

"Oh. Well, you're really gonna hate Fridays."

Insufficient Evidence

When a slick divorce lawyer arrived at the Pearly Gates, Saint Peter asked what he had done to deserve admission to Heaven.

"Well," said the lawyer, "just the other day I gave a dollar to a homeless man on the street."

"I'm glad to hear it," said Saint Peter, "but that's not enough to get you into Heaven. Is there anything else you've done that we should know about?"

"Sure," said the lawyer. "A few weeks ago, at Christmas-time, I gave a dollar to a Salvation Army bell ringer."

"Are these stories true?" Saint Peter asked his assistant.

"They are indeed," the assistant replied.

"In that case, what do you think we should do with this guy?"

"If you're asking my advice," said the assistant, "let's give him back his two bucks and tell him to go to Hell."

The Doctor and the Devil

A nasty and imperious physician is shocked to find himself in Hell.

"I don't belong here!" he tells the Devil. "I'm a doctor."

"I know," says the Devil. "And because you were a doctor and you did help some people, I'll give you a choice as to exactly which section of Hell you'll be going to."

He leads the doctor down the hall and points to a door. The doctor opens it and sees nothing but fire and brimstone. Slamming it shut, he says, "I'm certainly not going in there."

"Well, then," says the Devil, "how about the door on your right, number 211?"

When he opens that door, the doctor sees people being chased by wild animals.

"That one's just as bad," he says.

"Well, how about the door over there?" says the Devil.

When the doctor opens the third door, he sees a group of men with stethoscopes being served drinks by women in white. "Bingo!" he says. "That's the place for me!"

The Devil, who is clearly surprised, takes a peek inside. "My mistake," he says. "I'm sorry, but that one's not for you."

"Why not?"

"Because that's the Nurses' Hell."

It's a Wonderful Life

Two old and close friends make a pact that the first one to die will do everything within his power to contact the other. A few months later, Richard dies of a heart attack, leaving Pete lonely and depressed.

A month or so later, Pete answers the phone and it's Richard — just as he promised. "I'm so glad to hear from you," says Pete. "Boy, do I miss you! Tell me, what do you do all day?"

"I start off with a big breakfast. Then I have sex, and after that I lie in the sun. Then it's time for lunch, followed by a nap and more sex until it's time for dinner. And if I feel like it, I have sex one more time before I go to sleep."

"Really? That's fantastic! I had no idea that Heaven would be like that."

"Who said anything about Heaven? I'm a bull in Wisconsin!"

In 2015, many years after I first heard this one, a front-page article in the <u>Wall Street Journal</u>, datelined Shawano, Wisconsin, began, "Atop a wooded hill here in the heart of America's Dairyland, an industry legend was recently laid to rest. It wasn't some milk magnate or a famed innovator, but an ornery, 2,700-pound bull named Toystory—a titan of artificial insemination who sired an estimated 500,000 offspring in more than 50 countries."

Just Rewards

When Father Flannigan arrived at the entrance to Heaven, there was one man waiting in front of him. Saint Peter turned to him and said, "Bill McGuire?"

"That's me."

"It says here that you drove a taxi for thirty-four years."

"That's correct."

"Very well," said Saint Peter. "Take this golden scepter and put on this silk robe. Walk straight ahead and someone from the housing administration will assign you to a luxury apartment."

Turning next to the priest, Saint Peter said, "Father Flannigan, I presume?"

"Yes indeed."

"What would you say was your greatest accomplishment?"

"I have served the Lord all my life."

"Indeed you have, my good man, which is why we're happy to have you here. Please put on this cotton robe and carry this wooden staff, and you'll be assigned to one of our nicest dormitories."

"Saint Peter, with all due respect, there must be some mistake. Are you telling me that the taxi driver gets a silk robe and a golden scepter, and I, who did nothing but serve the Lord, receive only a cotton robe and a wooden staff?"

"I understand why you're puzzled," says Saint Peter. "But up here it's not only what you have done that counts, but how it affected other people. When you preached, people slept. But when that taxi driver drove, believe me, they prayed."

Terms and Conditions

Three nurses appear at the Pearly Gates. "Tell me," Saint Peter says to the first one. "What did you do on earth?"

"I was a birthing nurse. My job was to help bring precious little babies into the world."

"You may enter," says Saint Peter. Turning to the second nurse, he asks what she had done on earth.

"I worked in a trauma unit," she says. "I tried to save the lives of people who had been in bad accidents."

"You may enter," says Saint Peter.

When he asks the third nurse, she pauses for a moment and takes a deep breath. "I worked for an HMO," she says. "Over the years, I saved my company hundreds of thousands of dollars by refusing extended care to people who were trying to take advantage of the system."

"You, too, may enter," says Saint Peter.

"Thank you!" she says. "I can't believe you're allowing me in. Do you really mean it?"

"I do," says Saint Peter. "In fact, you've been preapproved. But you can only stay for three days."

In some versions Saint Peter adds, "And then you can go to Hell."

Curses!

A passionate golfer dies and is greeted by Saint Peter. "You have lived an exemplary life," Saint Peter says, "but according to our records, there was one occasion when you took the Lord's name in vain."

"Yes, I'm sorry to say that I remember it clearly," the golfer says. "Our club was having a tournament, and I was playing awfully well. When I reached the eighteenth hole, all I needed was an easy par-four to win the trophy. Unfortunately, my tee shot landed in a rough clump of grass."

"And that's when you took the Lord's name in vain?"

"No. I knew that if I hit the ball just right, I could probably reach the green. Unfortunately, the ball bounced back and ended up in the trap."

"So *that's* when you took the Lord's name in vain."

"No. I was frustrated, of course, but I kept my composure. I checked all the angles and shot very carefully, and the ball ended up just nine or ten inches from the cup."

"Oh, no," says Saint Peter. "Don't tell me you missed the goddamn putt!"

Too Good to Be True

Harold Bromberg had lived a saintly life. He was such a righteous man that when he died, the welcoming angel in Heaven couldn't believe what he was reading in Bromberg's file. "Honestly, I've never seen a life like this," the angel said. "Is it possible that you didn't commit a single sin?"

"Oh, I must have," said Bromberg. "But I did try my best to follow the rules of both God and man."

"It looks like you succeeded," said the angel. "So I'm going to send you back to earth for one night so you can commit a sin. Nothing terrible, but just enough so that when we bring you back here at midnight, your record will be a little more believable."

A moment later, Bromberg was back on earth – and very confused. How could he possibly commit a sin? But an order was an order, so he was determined to try. It was dinnertime, so he wandered into a restaurant, where the waitress seemed to be attracted to him. She was in her fifties and far from pretty, but when she began flirting with Bromberg, he did nothing to discourage her.

As she handed him the check, she said, "My shift ends in an hour. If you'd like to come back then, we could have a drink together. And who knows where that might lead?"

Harold had a pretty good idea of where that might lead, so he agreed to return in an hour. As he expected, the two of them ended up in his hotel room, where they got into bed together and enjoyed themselves immensely.

As Bromberg started to get dressed for his return trip to Heaven, the waitress smiled at him and said, "My dear Harold, this has been the most wonderful evening of my life. I've been alone for so many years. Do you have any idea what a *mitzvah* you did tonight?"

———

Depending on the audience, this joke could be told with a word or phrase other than <u>mitzvah</u>, *a Hebrew term that, when used in this way, means a good deed or an act of kindness.*

Coals to Newcastle

A wealthy man who was near death refused to believe the old adage that you can't take it with you. Having worked hard for his money and invested it wisely, he petitioned the Lord, asking if he could bring at least some of his wealth to his heavenly home.

An angel appeared to him and said, "I'm sorry, but when you die, you can't bring any of your possessions with you to Heaven."

The man respectfully pointed out that he had been exceedingly generous to the poor, and he asked the angel if he would please consult a higher authority. The following night the angel appeared to him again and said, "This has never happened before, but because of your many charitable acts, you will be allowed to bring one suitcase with you."

The man was delighted to hear this, and he thanked the angel profusely. He then filled his largest suitcase with gold bars and put it beside his bed.

A week later, the man died and appeared at the Pearly Gates with his suitcase.

"Just a minute," said Saint Peter. "You can't bring that in."

"Could you please check your records?" the man said. "I believe I have permission to bring in one bag."

It took a few minutes, but Saint Peter confirmed that the new arrival's information was correct. "I've never seen this before," he said, "but you're right – an exception has indeed been made for you. Would you please open the suitcase so I can see what you've got?"

Saint Peter was overcome with curiosity. What could possibly be so important that this man couldn't leave it behind?

A moment later, he had his answer. "I can't believe this," Saint Peter said. "You brought *pavement*?"

———

Some people have a slightly delayed response to this one because the brain has to go through an additional step to process it. And it's worth noting that in this case, at least, a rich man who is deeply attached to his own material wealth is still welcome in Heaven.

A Better Place?

When Malcolm died, he found himself in a beautiful place with all the pleasures and beauty he had dreamed of.

A figure in white approached him and said, "Malcolm, you are entitled to anything you want, and I'll do everything possible to make you happy."

For months, Malcolm enjoyed the heavenly music, wonderful meals, and, yes, lovely ladies.

After a while, Malcolm approached the figure in white. "I've really been enjoying myself," he said, "but now I'd like to accomplish something."

"What do you mean?"

"Well, I'd like to feel useful," Malcolm said. "I'd like to make a contribution. I'd like to do some *work*."

"I'm terribly sorry, but that's the one wish I am unable to grant. People here don't work. All they do is enjoy themselves."

"But a life of total pleasure is so boring," said Malcolm. "It has no meaning. I'm starting to think that maybe I'd be better off in Hell."

"My dear Malcolm, where do you think you are?"

––––––––

Whether or not this story qualifies as a joke, I like its bold challenge to the time-honored ideas and images of human happiness—and of Heaven.

ACKNOWLEDGMENTS

My wife, Linda, came up with the title *Die Laughing*, and had she done nothing else, it would have been enough. But naming the book was just the beginning. Together, amid much laughter, we reviewed every joke and cartoon to determine which ones deserved to make the final cut. Most of the better joke titles are hers as well, which seems only right for someone who still brags of having been named the wittiest member of her high school graduating class almost half a century later.

Our three sons — Ben (B.J.), Jesse, and Lev — were encouraging, supportive, and delighted that Dad had undertaken this project. As the Bible says, although I forget exactly where, Blessed is the man who is part of a funny family.

My friends Joel Leeman, Jeffrey Summit, and Jerry Samet spent many hours rating the jokes and suggesting some that I hadn't considered. Joel Leeman also took a heavy red pencil to my brief commentaries when he found them insufficiently interesting or insightful, which was alarmingly often. It's never easy to have your wisdom questioned, but Joel's judgment is close to impeccable.

Other friends and colleagues who deserve my thanks include (but are certainly not limited to) Steve Broder, Joel Segel, Debbie Zaitchik, Peter Waful, Bill Pappas, Cindy Shulak-Rome, Bob Boucher, Jim Block, Jim Pietsch, Gary

Rosenblatt, David Zises, Chris Miner, Jeff Gibson, Nancy Stieber, Larry Kushner, Howard Cooper, David Small, Art Vandelay, Barry Holtz, and the four funniest men I know: Don Witchel, Moshe Waldoks, Jonathan Katz, and the incomparable Jack Handey.

Turning now to the making of books, I'm fortunate to have worked with a group of professionals who do their work so effectively they make it look easy: Matthew Benjamin, my thoughtful and responsive editor; Richard Abate, my excellent agent; and the talented Cherlynne Li at Touchstone, who came up with such an engaging cover design. I am also grateful to Lara Blackman, Shida Carr, and Martha Schwartz, and to Susan Moldow, the publisher, who championed this book from the moment she heard about it. Kyle Tannler at The Cartoon Bank, who helped me review mass quantities of cartoons, was a joy to work with.

Finally, thank you to the ninety-odd people who voted for their favorite cartoons and will undoubtedly be reading this page to see if they are mentioned. I'm grateful for your help, and I wish I could remember your names!

ILLUSTRATION CREDITS

ABOUT THE AUTHOR

William Novak has written or coauthored some two dozen books, including the autobiographies of Lee Iacocca, Tip O'Neill, Nancy Reagan, Oliver North, the Mayflower Madam, Magic Johnson, Natan Sharansky, and Tim Russert. In an article about ghostwriters, the *New York Times* called him "the biggest name in the business." He is also the coeditor, with Moshe Waldoks, of *The Big Book of Jewish Humor* and *The Big Book of New American Humor*.

He and his wife live in the Boston area. They have three grown sons, all of whom are writers.